COPYCAT RECIPES COOKBOOK

101 RECIPES TO COOK YOUR FAVORITE RESTAURANTS' DISHES AT HOME IN A HEALTHY AND TASTY WAY

By
Lara Gray

© **Copyright 2019 - All rights reserved.**

The content contained within this book may not be reproduced, duplicated or transmitted without direct written permission from the author or the publisher.

Under no circumstances will any blame or legal responsibility be held against the publisher, or author, for any damages, reparation, or monetary loss due to the information contained within this book. Either directly or indirectly.

Legal Notice:

This book is copyright protected. This book is only for personal use. You cannot amend, distribute, sell, use, quote or paraphrase any part, or the content within this book, without the consent of the author or publisher.

Disclaimer Notice:

Please note the information contained within this document is for educational and entertainment purposes only. All effort has been executed to present accurate, up to date, and reliable, complete information. No warranties of any kind are declared or implied. Readers acknowledge that the author is not engaging in the rendering of legal, financial, medical or professional advice. The content within this book has been derived from various sources. Please consult a licensed professional before attempting any techniques outlined in this book.

By reading this document, the reader agrees that under no circumstances is the author responsible for any losses, direct or indirect, which are incurred as a result of the use of information contained within this document, including, but not limited to, — errors, omissions, or inaccuracies.

Table of Contents

INTRODUCTION 10

CHAPTER 1.

BREAKFAST 13

1. BACON GOUDA MUFFIN 13
2. EGGY BURRITO 14
3. FRENCH TOAST STICKS 17
4. HAM - EGG & CHEESE BISCUIT 19
5. PANCAKE PLATTER 22

CHAPTER 2.

MAINS 24

6. COPYCAT POPEYE'S BLACKENED CHICKEN TENDERS 24
7. PANDA EXPRESS BLACK PEPPER CHICKEN COPYCAT RECIPE 26
8. KETO FRIED CHICKEN TENDERS CHICK-FIL-A COPYCAT RECIPE 28
9. CHIMICHICKEN: CHIMICHURRI MARINATED CHICKEN 31

CHAPTER 3.

SIDES 34

10. CAFÉ RIO'S BLACK BEANS 34
11. EL CHARRO'S CHILE RELLENOS 35
12. ROSA MEXICANO'S MUSHROOM QUESADILLAS 38
13. ABUELO'S JALAPEÑO CHEESE FRITTERS 40
14. CHIPOTLE'S SOFRITAS 42
15. CAFÉ RIO'S FRESH FLOUR TORTILLAS 44

16. CHIPOTLE'S CILANTRO LIME RICE 46
17. EL TORITO'S SWEET CORN CAKE 47
18. ACAPULCO'S MEXICAN RICE 49
19. CHILI'S BLACK BEAN 50
20. TACO TIME'S BEAN BURRITO 52

CHAPTER 4.
SEAFOOD 54

21. RED LOBSTER'S GARLIC SHRIMP SCAMPI 54
22. BONEFISH GRILL'S BANG-BANG SHRIMP 55
23. CHI-CHI'S SEAFOOD CHIMICHANGA 57
24. RED LOBSTER'S COPYCAT LOBSTER PIZZA.......................59
25. BONEFISH GRILL'S SKEWERED SHRIMP WITH PAN-ASIAN GLAZE 61
26. DIY RED HOOK'S LOBSTER POUND 63
27. COPYCAT BUBBA GUM'S COCONUT SHRIMP 65
28. TONY ROMA'S GRILLED SALMON WITH CAROLINA HONEYS SAUCE 67
29. RED LOBSTER'S CAJUN SHRIMP 69
30. "APPLEBEE'S" HONEY GRILLED SALMON 70
31. "LONG JOHNS SILVER'S" BATTER-DIPPED FISH 72
32. "POPEYE'S" CAJUN FISH...74
33. "BONEFISH GRILL" PAN-FRIED TILAPIA WITH CHIMICHURRI SAUCE 76
34. LUBY'S BAKED FISH 77
35. "RUTH CHRIS STEAKHOUSE" SHRIMP ORLEANS 79

36. "Panda Express" Honey Walnut Shrimp 81

CHAPTER 5.
POULTRY 84

37. Cracker Barrel's Chicken Fried Chicken 84
38. Cracker Barrel's Broccoli Cheddar Chicken 86
39. Cracker Barrel's Grilled Chicken Tenderloin 87
40. Cracker Barrel's Sunday Chicken 88
41. Cracker Barrel's Creamy Chicken and Rice 90
42. Cracker Barrel's Campfire Chicken 91
43. Cracker Barrel's Chicken and Dumplings 93
44. Red Lobster's Classic BBQ Chicken 95
45. Chipotle's Grilled Sweet Chili Lime Chicken 96
46. Chipotle's Adobo Chicken 98
47. Chipotle's Classic Grilled Chicken 100
48. Panda Express' Orange Chicken 101
49. Chick-fil-A Chicken Nuggets with Honey Mustard Dip   104
50. Boneless Buffalo Wings 106
51. Chicken Quesadilla 108
52. Pei Wei's Sesame Chicken 110
53. Pei Wei's Coconut Curry with Chicken 113

CHAPTER 6.
MEAT 116

54. Southwest Steak 116

55.	DIY Sizzling Steak, Cheese, and Mushrooms Skillet 118	
56.	Outback Style Steak	120
57.	Teriyaki Filet Medallions	122
58.	Beef Stew	124
59.	Meat Loaf	126
60.	Roast Beef	127
61.	Grilled Pork Chops	129
62.	Peppered Ribeye Steaks	131
63.	Mushroom Braised Pot Roast	133
64.	Outback Steak House Grilled Pork chops	134
65.	Holiday Inn Victorville Pork Egg Roll in a Bowl 136	
66.	Fudpuckers Bacon-wrapped Tuna	138
67.	Tojo's Bar and Grill Orange Roast Pork Loin Recipe 140	

CHAPTER 7.
VEGETABLES 143

68.	Five Cheese Ziti Al Forno	143
69.	Ravioli di Portobello	145
70.	Eggplant Parmigiana	148
71.	Gnocchi with Spicy Tomato and Wine Sauce	150

CHAPTER 8.
SOUPS & STEWS 153

72.	Outback's French Onion Soup	153
73.	Red Lobster's Clam Chowder	154

74.	CARRABBA'S MAMA MANDOLA SICILIAN CHICKEN SOUP	156
75.	CARRABBA'S SAUSAGE AND LENTIL SOUP	158
76.	DENNY'S VEGETABLE AND BEEF BARLEY SOUP	160

CHAPTER 9.
SNACKS 162

77.	TACO BELL BEAN BURRITO	162
78.	TACO BELL BEEFY 5-LAYER BURRITO	164
79.	TACO BELL CHICKEN BURRITO	166
80.	TACO BELL CHEESE POTATO BURRITO	169
81.	TACO BELL BLACK BEAN BURRITO	171
82.	TACO BELL CHILI CHEESE BURRITO	173
83.	TACO BELL CRUNCHY TACO	175
84.	TACO BELL NACHO SUPREME	176
85.	TACO BELL BURRITO SUPREME	178

CHAPTER 10.
DESSERTS 181

86.	DISNEY'S FAMOUS CHURROS	181
87.	TROLLY TREATS CHURRO TOFFEE	183
88.	RICE CEREAL TREATS	184
89.	GERMAN PAVILION CARAMEL CORN	186
90.	GINGER BREAD POPCORN	188
91.	PORT ORLEANS BEIGNETS	190
92.	PINEAPPLE UPSIDE DOWN CAKES	192
93.	LIBERTY TREE TAVERN OOEY GOOEY TOFFEE CAKE	194
94.	TRIPLE CHOCOLATE MELTDOWN	196

95.	CHOCOLATE MOUSSE DESSERT SHOOTER	198
96.	CINNAMON APPLE TURNOVER	200
97.	CHERRY CHOCOLATE COBBLER	202
98.	CHOCOLATE PECAN PIE	204
99.	PUMPKIN CUSTARD WITH GINGERSNAPS	205
100.	PEACH COBBLER	208
101.	ROYAL DANSK BUTTER COOKIES	209

CONCLUSION **212**

Introduction

Copycat meals or recipes have become very known and popular with the restaurant's ever-high cost of eating.

To begin with, a copycat is an elementary word. It is used to imitate or replicate something done by a person or group of people. It is also used to describe the act of fraud or identification or duplication of someone or something's look. It is also used as the act of imitating or copying something; an exact representation especially in appearance or gesture. The term is also used for something very similar to another.

Most of the time, the word is used when it comes to food. More specifically, desserts. Copycat recipes are top-rated because they are very cheap to make, and the ingredients used are simple and very available. It is also famous as it is the right way of making use of ingredients or food that anyone does not consume. It is also famous for this reason as it helps in recycling the food.

If you have always wanted to cook your favorite restaurant dishes at home without spending a fortune, it's now possible with the help of this cookbook. The recipes are designed to re-create restaurant recipes many people believe would be too complicated to make at home. With easy step-by-step instructions, helpful hints, and easy to follow you can prepare top restaurant dishes in no time.

- 100%-Very Easy Recipes-

- Eliminate expensive and complicated restaurant recipes-

- Tested and approved by home cooks-

- Get the restaurant-quality meal you're craving without the price tag-

- Save time and money-

- Never worry about over-ordering again! -

All dishes are broken down according to course and are carefully written in enough detail to duplicate the pros' exact meal. A rule of thumb, this book has been reported in a more straightforward way. The exciting thing is that the meals in the book are simple, easy to make and inexpensive. They are quick to come off the griddle and grill and require minimal prep work. They have been tested on various men and women, and there is no doubt that they have all enjoyed whatever meal was cooked.

Cooking top secret recipes from restaurants will also make your friends and family wonder where you've learned to cook so well. Imagine cooking a whole meal that looks like it was the restaurant's takeout food. We bet some friends of yours won't even believe you've cooked it! So, hurry! Go to your kitchen and start cooking. Enjoy, and have fun!

Inside you'll find recipes for over seventy popular restaurant meals. Most of them don't take long to prepare and you may already have some of the ingredients in your cupboard. These recipes are delicious. Enjoy!

Chapter 1. Breakfast

1. Bacon Gouda Muffin

Preparation time: 15 minutes

Cooking time: 20 minutes

Servings: 2

Ingredients:

- 2 English muffins
- 2 Eggs
- 2 tbsp Half & half
- 4 slices Bacon
- 1 tbsp Butter - divided
- 2-4 small pieces Smoked Gouda cheese
- Pepper & salt, as desired

Directions:

1. Warm the oven to reach 350° Fahrenheit.
2. Slice the bacon pieces into halves and bake for 20 minutes until browned.
3. Whisk the eggs and Half and Half and dump the eggs onto a med-low hot griddle. Do not move the eggs until they are almost done and fold them into smaller portions.
4. Toast the muffin and add butter to both sides.
5. Prepare the sandwich with eggs on the bottom bun, followed by cheese and the bacon. Add the top and serve.

Nutrition:

Calories: 380

Carbs: 22g

Fat: 22g

Protein: 21g

2. Eggy Burrito

Preparation time: 20 minutes

Cooking time: 5 hours & 20 minutes

Servings: 10

Ingredients:

- 1 lb. bulk Pork sausage
- .5 lb. Bacon strips
- 18 Large eggs
- 2 cups Frozen hash brown shredded potatoes
- 1 large - chopped Onion
- 1 can - undiluted - 10.75 oz. condensed - cheddar cheese soup
- 4 oz, can - chopped Green chilies
- .5 tsp Pepper
- 1 tsp Garlic powder
- 2 cups Shredded cheddar cheese
- 10 - 10-inch Warmed flour tortillas

Optional Toppings:

- Salsa
- Hot pepper sauce
- Jalapeno peppers

Directions:

1. Mix the sausage, bacon, hash browns, eggs, onions, soup, chilies, pepper, and garlic powder.

2. Thaw and shred the hash browns. Cook and drain the sausage and bacon on a layer of paper towels. Whisk and add the eggs with the bacon, sausage, potatoes, onion, and soup.

3. Add about half of the egg mixture into the cooker coated with a cooking oil spray. Top the mix and reserve half of the cheese. Repeat the layers.

4. Cook, covered, using the low function for four to five hours or until the center is set.

5. Spoon about ¾ cup of egg mixture into the middle part of the tortilla.

6. Fold the bottom and sides of the tortilla over the filling and roll it up.

7. Add toppings of your choice.

Nutrition:

Calories: 290

Carbs: 21g

Fat: 17g

Protein: 14g

3. French Toast Sticks

Preparation time: 15 minutes

Cooking time: 40 minutes

Servings: 1.5 dozen

Ingredients:

- 6 day-olds Texas toast slices
- 4 Large eggs
- 1 cup 2% milk
- .25-.5 tsp Cinnamon
- 2 tbsp Sugar
- 1 tsp Vanilla extract

Optional Ingredients:

- 1 cup Crushed cornflakes
- Confectioner's sugar
- Maple syrup

Directions:

1. Slice each piece of bread into thirds and arrange them in an ungreased pan.
2. Whisk the milk, sugar, eggs, vanilla, and cinnamon. Pour it over the bread and soak for about two minutes, flipping once. Coat the dough with cornflake crumbs.
3. Place in a greased baking pan. Freeze the sticks until firm (45 min.). Store in the freezer.
4. When it's time to eat, add and bake them at 425 °Fahrenheit for eight minutes. Flip them over and cook f until golden brown (10-12 min.).
5. Sprinkle them using the confectioners' sugar and serve with syrup.

Nutrition:

Calories: 380

Carbs: 49g

Fat: 18g

Protein: 5g

4. Ham - Egg & Cheese Biscuit

Preparation time: 15 minutes

Cooking time: 30 minutes

Servings: 10

Ingredients:

- 1 cup Fully cooked ham
- 1 tsp Coarsely ground pepper - divided
- 1 cup Shredded cheddar cheese
- 4 cups Biscuit baking mix
- 1 cup 2% milk
- 3 tbsp Butter

For the Eggs:

- 2 tbsp Butter
- .5 cup 2% milk
- 8 large eggs
- .125 tsp Salt
- .25 tsp Black pepper - coarsely ground
- 1 cup Shredded cheddar cheese

Optional Toppings:

- Sliced tomato
- Red onion
- Salsa
- Avocado

Directions:

1. Chop the ham and green peppers. Warm the oven to reach 425° Fahrenheit.
2. Measure and add the biscuit mix, cheese, ham, and ½ teaspoon of the pepper into a large mixing container. Pour in the milk, stirring until it's just moistened.

3. Scoop it out onto a lightly floured surface, then knead it gently about eight to ten times. Work the dough until it's about a one-inch thickness. Use a floured biscuit cutter to make a 2.5-inch biscuit.

4. Arrange the prepared biscuits about two inches apart on an ungreased baking sheet. Brush with melted butter and dust using the rest of the pepper.

5. Bake the buttered biscuits until golden brown (12-14 min.). Mix the eggs with the milk, pepper, plus salt.

6. Warm a large non-stick skillet using the medium temperature setting to melt the butter.

7. Dump the egg mixture into the pan, stirring until the eggs are thickened and no liquid egg remains. Mix in the cheese and move the pan to a cool burner.

8. Slice the warm biscuits into halves. Layer the bottoms with the egg mixture and toppings as desired. Replace the tops and serve.

Nutrition:

Calories: 370

Carbs: 30g

Fat: 21g

Protein: 16g

5. Pancake Platter

Preparation time: 15 minutes

Cooking time: 20 minutes

Servings: 2.5 dozen

Ingredients:

- 1.5 tsp Baking powder
- 4 cups A-P flour
- 2 tsp Baking soda
- .25 cup Sugar
- 2 tsp Salt
- 4 large eggs
- 4 cups Buttermilk

Directions:

1. Whisk the baking soda, flour, salt, baking powder, and sugar.

2. Use another container to beat the buttermilk and room temperature eggs. Mix it into the dry fixings.

3. Pour the batter (¼ cup each) onto a lightly greased hot griddle. Flip each of the cakes once bubbles appear.

4. Flip and continue cooking until they're done. Garnish with your favorite toppings and serve.

Nutrition:

Calories: 440

Carbs: 71g

Fat: 16g

Protein: 5g

Chapter 2. Mains

6. Copycat Popeye's Blackened Chicken Tenders

Preparation time: 7 minutes

Cooking time: 18 minutes

Servings: 4

Ingredients:

- 2 tsp Sea Salt
- 2 tsp Smoked Paprika
- 1 tsp Cayenne Pepper
- 2 tsp Chili Powder
- 2 tsp Garlic Powder
- 1-2 tsp Black Pepper

- 2 lbs. Chicken Breast Tenderloin
- 1 tbsp Vegetable Oil

Directions:

1. Warm the oven to 350 degrees.
2. Mix all seasonings into one seasoning blend (blackened seasoning) in a small bowl.
3. Put seasonings plus the chicken in a large freezer bag; shake, then massage.
4. Warm the vegetable oil in a large cast-iron skillet within 2-3 minutes on medium-high heat.
5. Put the tender, then cook within 3-4 minutes each side.
6. Move it to the oven, and allow to cook for an additional ten minutes.

Nutrition:

Calories: 420

Fat: 12g

Cholesterol: 193mg

Sodium: 1343mg

Carbohydrates: 3g

Protein: 71g

7. Panda Express Black Pepper Chicken Copycat Recipe

Preparation time: 5 minutes

Cooking time: 25 minutes

Servings: 6

Ingredients:

For the Chicken:

- 6 chicken thighs, boneless, skinless
- 1 green bell pepper, diced
- 1 yellow onion, sliced
- 3 celery stalks, sliced
- 2 tbsp corn starch
- 1 tbsp garlic powder
- 1 tsp cracked black pepper

- 1/2 tbsp onion powder
- 2 cups cooked rice
- 1 tsp ginger powder
- 2 tbsp peanut oil

For the Sauce:

- 1/2 cup chicken broth
- 1/4 cup oyster sauce
- 1/4 cup rice wine vinegar
- 1/2 tbsp garlic, minced
- 1 tsp black pepper
- 1 tsp chili powder
- 1/2 tsp ginger powder

Directions:

1. Mix sauce fixings in a large bowl then set aside.
2. Pat dry the chicken and cut it into 1" cubes.
3. Place your chicken in a large bowl, then mix in the cornstarch, pepper, plus salt.
4. Warm the peanut oil on medium heat in a skillet.
5. Put the chicken in oil in small batches so it can cook quickly.
6. Return all the chicken into the pan and add vegetables, sauté within 5 minutes.

7. Put the sauce and broth into a pan, boil, adjust the heat, and simmer within 10 minutes.

8. Serve on top of a large bowl of rice and enjoy!

Nutrition:

Calories: 406

Fat: 5g

Cholesterol: 110mg

Sodium: 440mg

Carbohydrates: 25g

Fiber: 2g

Sugar: 2g

Protein: 21g

8. Keto Fried Chicken Tenders Chick-Fil-A Copycat Recipe

Preparation time: 10 minutes

Cooking time: 15 minutes

Servings: 8

Ingredients:

- 8 Chicken Tenders
- 24 oz Jar of Dill Pickles juice
- 3/4 Cup Now Foods Almond Flour
- 1 teaspoon salt
- 1 teaspoon Pepper
- 2 Eggs, beaten
- 1 1/2 Cups pork panko
- Nutiva Organic Coconut Oil for frying

Low Carb Copycat Chick-Fil-A Sauce:

- 1/2 Cup Mayo
- 2 tsp Yellow Mustard
- 1 tsp Lemon Juice

- 2 tbs Honey Trees Sugar-Free Honey
- 1 tbs Primal Kitchen Classic BBQ Sauce

Directions:

1. Marinade the chicken tenders in the pickle juice, put it in a large zip lock bag within 1 hour or overnight.
2. Whisk almond flour, salt, plus pepper in a small bowl.
3. Prepare three bowls, the first one with almond flour mixture, then the second bowl is the eggs, and the third bowl is the pork panko.
4. Put the chicken in the almond flour bowl, then in the egg, and finally in the pork panko until well coated.
5. Put 2 inches coconut oil in a pan on medium-high heat.
6. When the oil is hot, put tenders in the oil and cook about 3 minutes on each side or until golden brown.

Low Carb Copycat Chick-Fil-A Sauce:

1. Mix all sauce fixings and stir until thoroughly combined in a small bow.

Nutrition:

Calories: 193.6

Fat: 9 g

Carbs: 1.6 g

Sugar: .5 g

Protein: 26.8 g

9. Chimichicken: Chimichurri Marinated Chicken

Preparation time: 10 minutes

Cooking time: 40 minutes

Servings: 6

Ingredients:

- 6 bone-in, skin-on chicken thighs
- 2 medium sweet potatoes, chopped

- 1 small onion, diced
- 2 tablespoon extra-virgin olive oil

For the marinade:

- 1 bunch fresh flat-leaf parsley
- 1/2 bunch fresh cilantro
- 3 tbsp fresh oregano leaves
- 8 to 10 medium garlic cloves
- 2 teaspoon unrefined salt
- 1/4 cup extra-virgin olive oil
- 1/4 cup red wine vinegar
- juice of 1 lime

Directions:

1. For the marinade, puree all of the fixings in a food processor.
2. Massage each thigh with about 1 tablespoon of the marinade.
3. Marinate in the fridge overnight.
4. Warm the oven at 425F. Put the chopped sweet potatoes plus onion in a single layer on a sheet pan and stir with the 2 tablespoons of EVOO. Sprinkle with salt. Put the thighs on top.

5. Bake within 40-45 minutes. Serve with the remaining EVOO and red wine vinegar.

Nutrition:

Calories: 542

Carbs: 68g

Fat: 15g

Protein: 37g

Chapter 3.   Sides

10.   Café Rio's Black Beans

Preparation time: 10 minutes

Cooking time: 30 minutes

Servings: 8

Ingredients:

- 2 tablespoons olive oil
- 3 cloves garlic, minced
- 1 jalapeño pepper, minced
- 2 (15-ounce) cans black beans (one can drain, one with liquid)
- 2 teaspoons cumin

- 12 ounces tomato juice
- 1 teaspoon salt
- ½ teaspoon black pepper
- ¼ cup chopped cilantro

Directions:

1. Warm the oil and sauté the garlic and jalapeño until fragrant in a large non-stick skillet over medium heat.
2. Add the beans and cumin. Simmer and cook within 5–10 minutes, until some of the liquid has evaporated.
3. Stir in the tomato juice, salt, pepper, and cilantro. Cook to heat through, and serve.

Nutrition:

Calories: 90

Carbs: 16g

Fat: 0g

Protein: 6g

11. El Charro's Chile Rellenos

Preparation time: 15 minutes

Cooking time: 40 minutes

Servings: 4

Ingredients:

For the chilies:

- 8 fresh green chilies
- 2 cups shredded cheddar
- 2 cups Monterey Jack cheese, shredded

For the batter:

- 3 eggs
- 3 tablespoons flour
- 1 teaspoon salt
- 1 teaspoon black pepper

For topping (optional):

- 4 cups taco sauce, warmed
- 1 cup shredded cheddar
- 1 cup shredded Monterey Jack cheese
- Oil for frying

Directions:

1. Slice and core the peppers, leaving the stems on if possible. Stuff them with a mixture of the two kinds of cheese. Close the peppers around the cheese.
2. Heat the oil to 350°F.

3. Divide the eggs yolk and egg whites, then beat the whites until stiff.

4. Beat the egg yolks and fold them into the whites, together with the flour, salt, and pepper.

5. Dip the peppers into the batter and carefully lower them into the hot oil. Cook on each side until they are crisp and golden.

6. Heat the broiler to medium.

7. If desired, arrange the fried chilies in a baking pan and pour the warm taco sauce over them. Put on top the rest of the cheese and broil until the cheese is melted and bubbly.

Nutrition:

Calories: 290

Carbs: 4g

Fat: 29g

Protein: 10g

12. Rosa Mexicano's Mushroom Quesadillas

Preparation time: 10 minutes

Cooking time: 20 minutes

Servings: 6

Ingredients:

- 3 tablespoons olive oil
- 12 ounces mixed mushrooms (cremini, portobello, shiitake, oyster), trimmed and thinly sliced
- 1 medium white onion, finely chopped
- 2 cloves garlic, minced
- 2 serrano chilies, seeded, cored, and minced
- ¼ teaspoon salt
- 1 ½ cups shredded cheese (queso

chihuahua, Monterey Jack, or cheddar)

- 6 (6-inch) fresh corn tortillas

- Optional sour cream and salsa Verde, for serving

Directions:

1. In a medium skillet, warm the oil over medium-high heat until it shimmers. Add the mushrooms, onion, garlic, and chilies. Season with salt.

2. Cook within 8–10 minutes, or until the mushrooms are browned.

3. Transfer the filling mixture to a bowl and wipe out the skillet. Reduce the heat to medium-low.

4. Divide the cheese among the tortillas leaving a small gap around the edges. Spoon filling over half the tortilla and fold one side over the filling.

5. In batches, place the quesadillas in the hot skillet and cook on both sides until golden and crisp.

6. Serve with sour cream plus salsa Verde, if desired.

Nutrition:

Calories: 352

Carbs: 0g

Fat: 19g

Protein: 33g

13. Abuelo's Jalapeño Cheese Fritters

Preparation time: 15 minutes

Cooking time: 15 minutes

Servings: 40

Ingredients:

- 4 ounces cream cheese, softened
- 6 cups shredded cheddar cheese
- 6 cups shredded Monterey Jack cheese
- 4 fresh jalapeños, deseeded and finely chopped
- ½ teaspoon Lawry's seasoning
- Oil for frying
- 2 tablespoons all-purpose flour
- 2 eggs
- ½ cup of water
- 3 cups breadcrumbs
- Ranch dressing, for serving

Directions:

1. Mix the cream cheese, shredded cheeses, jalapeños, and seasoning in a mixing bowl.

2. Shape the mixture into balls using one level tablespoon for each. Place the balls on a baking sheet and set it in the fridge.

3. Heat the frying oil to 360°F. Set out a large baking sheet with a sheet of parchment and a platter with a paper towel.

4. Prepare your dipping station. In one bowl, place the flour. In the other bowl, whisk the eggs and mix in the water. Pour the breadcrumbs into a small baking pan or casserole dish.

5. Remove the cheese balls from the fridge. Working in small batches of 5–10 balls, drop them in the flour and toss to coat.

6. Then, coat them with egg and then breadcrumbs. Repeat the egg and breadcrumbs, and set them on the parchment-lined sheet.

7. Fry the cheese balls in batches for 1 to 1 ½ minute, or until they are golden brown. Drain on a paper towel. Ensure to let the oil heat up again before adding more cheese balls.

8. Serve immediately with ranch dressing.

Nutrition:

Calories: 1250

Carbs: 71g

Fat: 88g

Protein: 37g

14. Chipotle's Sofritas

Preparation time: 10 minutes

Cooking time: 25 minutes

Servings: 2

Ingredients:

- Sofritas
- 1 tablespoon avocado or olive oil
- ½ medium onion, diced
- 2 garlic cloves, minced
- 1 tsp chipotle chili in adobo sauce
- 1 tablespoon mild Hatch chili, diced
- 1 tablespoon Mexican Spice Mix
- 2 tablespoons tomato paste
- 1 package (16-ounces), organic extra firm tofu, drained, dried, crumbled
- 1 cup of your favorite Mexican beer
- Salt and black pepper to taste

- Tortillas and lime wedges for garnish

Mexican Spice Mix:

- ½ teaspoon dried oregano leaves
- 2 teaspoons ancho chili powder, ground
- 1 teaspoon cumin, ground
- ½ teaspoon coriander, ground
- ½ teaspoon kosher salt

Directions:

1. Place all the Mexican Spice Mix ingredients in a container or plastic bag and shake to mix.
2. Cook the onion plus garlic in oil on medium heat for 5 minutes.
3. Mix in both the chilies and the spice mix and sauté for another minute.
4. Pour in the tomato paste and cook for a minute.
5. Add the rest of the ingredients and cook for 5 more minutes.
6. Transfer the mixture to a bowl, and then serve with tortillas and thin lime wedges.

Nutrition:

Calories: 145

Carbs: 0g

Fat: 10g

Protein: 8g

15. Café Rio's Fresh Flour Tortillas

Preparation time: 1 hour & 10 minutes

Cooking time: 10 minutes

Servings: 6

Ingredients:

- 3 cups all-purpose flour
- 1 teaspoon salt
- 2 teaspoons baking powder
- ¾ cup lard (or shortening)
- ¾ cup boiling water

Directions:

1. Mix the flour, baking powder, plus salt in a mixing bowl.
2. Cut or rub in the lard (or shortening) until the mixture is evenly crumbly.

3. Put the water and stir until the dough comes together.

4. Turn the dough out onto a lightly floured surface and knead until smooth.

5. Put the dough in a bowl, lightly oiled, covered, then let it sit for one hour.

6. Divide the dough into the number and size of tortillas you want (6 large or 12 small).

7. Heat a skillet or tortilla Comal over medium-high heat. Dampen a clean towel and set out a plate.

8. Form the dough into balls and roll them out thin. You can cut around a plate for a perfect circle.

9. Cook the tortillas for about 1 minute on each side, until the dough is cooked and there are golden spots.

10. Remove the cooked tortilla to the plate and cover it with the towel while you prepare the rest.

Nutrition:

Calories: 180

Carbs: 18g

Fat: 3g

Protein: 3g

16. Chipotle's Cilantro Lime Rice

Preparation time: 5 minutes

Cooking time: 25 minutes

Servings: 6

Ingredients:

- 1 tablespoon vegetable oil
- 1 cup white basmati rice
- 2 tablespoons lime juice
- 1 ½ cups water
- 1 teaspoon salt
- 1 tablespoon fresh cilantro, chopped

Directions:

1. Warm t the oil and add the rice and lime juice in a 2-quart saucepan. Cook and stir for one or two minutes.

2. Add the water and salt. Boil and then lessen the heat and cover.
3. Simmer within 25–30 minutes until the water is absorbed.
4. Fluff it, and stir in the cilantro. Serve.

Nutrition:

Calories: 201

Carbs: 37g

Fat: 3g

Protein: 4g

17. El Torito's Sweet Corn Cake

Preparation time: 10 minutes

Cooking time: 25 minutes

Servings: 6

Ingredients:

- ¼ cup butter
- 2 tablespoons shortening
- ½ cup masa harina
- ¼ cup of cold water
- 10 ounces creamed corn

- 3 tablespoons cornmeal
- 3 tablespoons heavy cream
- ¼ cup of sugar
- ½ teaspoon baking powder
- ¼ teaspoon salt

Directions:

1. Preheat the oven to 350°F. Butter an 8-inch pan (round or square) that will fit inside a roasting pan.
2. Mix the butter plus the shortening until they are fluffy in a mixing bowl.
3. Gradually incorporate the masa harina, and then the water. Mix in the corn.
4. Mix the cornmeal, sugar, heavy cream, baking powder, and salt in a separate bowl.
5. Add the corn mixture to the other ingredients and mix just to combine.
6. Spread the batter in the prepared dish.
7. Place it in the roasting pan, then pour hot water in until it's about an inch deep.
8. Bake within 45–50 minutes until a toothpick inserted in the center comes out clean.

Nutrition:

Calories: 100

Carbs: 22g

Fat: 1g

Protein: 1g

18. Acapulco's Mexican Rice

Preparation time: 10 minutes

Cooking time: 55 minutes

Servings: 6

Ingredients:

- 3 tablespoons lard or chicken fat
- 1 large onion, diced
- 2 cups long-grain rice
- 2 cups chicken broth
- 1 cup tomato juice
- 1 cup diced tomatoes
- 1 tablespoon chopped parsley
- 2 cloves garlic, minced
- ½ teaspoon paprika
- ½ teaspoon ground cumin
- 1 teaspoon salt
- 1 dash white pepper

Directions:

1. Warm the oven to 350°F and butter a casserole dish.

2. In a skillet, melt the lard or chicken fat. Cook the onion and rice until they are lightly browned, about 10 minutes, stirring constantly. Transfer them to the prepared dish.

3. In the skillet, combine the remaining ingredients and bring them to a boil. Pour them over the rice and mix.

4. Covered it with foil and baked within 25–30 minutes. Fluff with a fork, and serve.

Nutrition:

Calories: 199

Carbs: 29g

Fat: 8g

Protein: 3g

19. Chili's Black Bean

Preparation time: 5 minutes

Cooking time: 25 minutes

Servings: 6

Ingredients:

- 2 cans (15.5-ounces each) black beans
- ½ teaspoon sugar
- 1 teaspoon ground cumin
- 1 teaspoon chili powder
- ½ teaspoon garlic powder
- 2 tablespoon red onion, diced finely
- ½ teaspoon fresh cilantro, minced (optional)
- ½ cup of water
- Salt and black pepper to taste
- Pico de Gallo and or sour cream for garnish (optional)

Directions:

1. Combine the beans, sugar, cumin, chili powder, garlic, onion, cilantro (if using), and water in a saucepan and mix well.
2. Over medium-low heat, let the bean mixture simmer for about 20-25 minutes—season with salt and pepper to taste.
3. Remove the beans from heat and transfer to serving bowls.
4. Garnish with Pico de Gallo or a dollop of sour cream, if desired.

Nutrition:

Calories: 320

Carbs: 53g

Fat: 8g

Protein: 14g

20. Taco Time's Bean Burrito

Preparation time: 15 minutes

Cooking time: 2 minutes

Servings: 6

Ingredients:

- 6 (10-inch) flour tortillas
- 2 cups pinto beans, mashed and warmed
- 1 cup brown or Mexican rice
- 1 cup shredded cheddar
- 2 cups chopped lettuce
- 2 tomatoes, diced
- ¾ cup guacamole
- ½ cup slaw mix
- ¼ cup ranch dressing

Directions:

1. To assemble the burritos, first, warm the tortillas.

2. Spread each with beans and add rice. Top with cheddar, lettuce, tomatoes, guacamole, slaw mix, and ranch dressing. Roll, and serve!

Nutrition:

Calories: 548

Carbs: 79g

Fat: 14g

Protein: 23g

Chapter 4. Seafood

21. Red Lobster's Garlic Shrimp Scampi

Preparation time: 15 minutes

Cooking time: 15 minutes

Servings: 4

Ingredients:

- 1-pound shrimp, peeled and deveined
- Salt and pepper to taste
- 1 tablespoon olive oil
- 3 garlic cloves, finely chopped
- 1½ white wine
- 2 tablespoons lemon juice
- ¼ teaspoon dried basil
- ¼ teaspoon dried oregano
- ¼ teaspoon dried rosemary
- ¼ teaspoon dried thyme
- ½ cup butter
- 2 tablespoons parsley leaves, minced
- ¼ cup Parmesan cheese, shredded (optional)

Directions:

1. Flavor shrimp with salt and pepper.

2. In a pan with heated oil, sauté shrimp on medium-high heat for about 2 minutes or until color changes to pink. Transfer onto a plate and set aside.

3. In the same pan, sauté garlic for 30 seconds or until aromatic. Pour in white wine plus lemon juice, stir, then bring to a boil.

4. Adjust heat to medium-low and cook for an additional 4 minutes. Mix in basil, oregano, rosemary, and thyme.

5. Then, add butter gradually. Mix until completely melted and blended with other ingredients. Remove from heat.

6. Return shrimp to pan and add parsley.

7. Sprinkle Parmesan on top, if desired. Serve.

Nutrition:

Calories 448

Fat 29 g

Carbs 3 g

Protein 26 g

Sodium 362 mg

22. Bonefish Grill's Bang-Bang Shrimp

Preparation time: 5 minutes

Cooking time: 5 minutes

Servings: 4

Ingredients:

- ½ cup mayonnaise
- ¼ cup Thai sweet chili sauce
- 3-5 drops hot chili sauce
- ½ cup cornstarch
- 1-pound small shrimp, peeled and deveined
- 1½ cups of vegetable oil

Directions:

1. To make the sauce, combine mayonnaise with Thai chili sauce and hot chili sauce in a bowl.
2. In a separate bowl, add cornstarch. Toss shrimp in cornstarch until well-coated.
3. Heat oil in a wok. Fry the shrimp within 2-3 minutes.
4. Transfer it into a plate lined with paper towels to drain excess oil. Serve shrimp in a bowl with sauce drizzled on top.

Nutrition:

Calories 274

Fat 11 g

Carbs 26 g

Protein 16 g

Sodium 1086 mg

23. Chi-Chi's Seafood Chimichanga

Preparation time: 10 minutes

Cooking time: 30 minutes

Servings: 6

Ingredients:

- 4 tablespoons butter
- 4 tablespoons flour
- ½ teaspoon butter
- 2 dashes black pepper, ground
- 2 cups of milk
- 8 ounces jack cheese, shredded
- 1 tablespoon dried parsley flakes
- ¼ teaspoon onion powder
- 1 16-ounce package crab meat, flaked
- 1 cup cottage cheese
- ¼ cup Parmesan cheese
- 1 egg
- 1 tablespoon lemon juice
- Shredded lettuce for serving

- ¼ cup sliced green onions for garnish

Directions:

1. Preheat oven to 375°F.
2. To make the sauce, heat butter in a pan on medium heat. Add flour, salt, and pepper. Mix, then pour in the milk. Stirring often, cook until sauce is thick, then simmer for an additional 1 minute.
3. Turn off heat and stir in jack cheese until thoroughly blended into the sauce.
4. In a bowl, combine crab meat, cottage and Parmesan cheese, egg, parsley, and onion powder. Warm the tortillas in the microwave within 10 seconds or until warm.
5. Wet the bottom side of the tortilla and add crab meat mixture on top. Fold tortilla to wrap filling.
6. Coat baking sheet with cooking spray. Bake chimichangas for about 25 minutes.
7. Reheat sauce until warm. Mix in lemon juice and stir until blended.
8. Transfer chimichangas to plates over a bed of shredded lettuce, if desired. Top with sauce and garnish with green onions before serving.

Nutrition:

Calories 794

Fat 33 g

Carbs 77 g

Protein 44 g

Sodium 1932 mg

24. Red Lobster's Copycat Lobster Pizza

Preparation time: 15 minutes

Cooking time: 5 minutes

Servings: 1

Ingredients:

- 1 10-inch flour tortillas
- 1-ounce roasted garlic butter

- 2 tablespoons Parmesan cheese, shredded
- 1/2 cup fresh Roma tomatoes, finely chopped
- 2 tbsp fresh basil, thin strips
- 2 ounces of lobster meat, chopped
- ½ cup Italian cheese blend, grated
- Vegetable oil for coating
- Dash salt and pepper
- Fresh lemon juice for serving

Directions:

1. Preheat oven to 450°F.
2. Coat one side of tortilla with garlic butter. Top with Parmesan cheese, tomatoes, basil, lobster meat, and Italian cheese blend in that order. Set aside.
3. Prepare a pizza pan. Grease with vegetable oil and cover with a dash of salt and pepper. Transfer pizza onto the pan. Bake for about 5 minutes.
4. Slice and drizzle with lemon juice. Serve.

Nutrition:

Calories 339

Fat 10 g

Carbs 41 g

Protein 22 g

Sodium 890 mg

25. Bonefish Grill's Skewered Shrimp with Pan-Asian Glaze

Preparation time: 5 minutes

Cooking time: 10 minutes

Servings: 4

Ingredients:

- ¼ ketchup
- ¼ cup oyster sauce
- 1 tablespoon soy sauce
- 1 tablespoon water
- ¾ tablespoon lemon juice
- 1 tablespoon extra-virgin olive oil, plus more
- 1 tbsp fresh ginger, chopped
- 1 tablespoon sugar
- 1 tablespoon honey
- 1-pound shrimp, peeled, deveined, and skewered

Directions:

1. In a bowl, add ketchup, oyster sauce, soy sauce, water, and lemon juice. Mix well.

2. Put olive oil in a deep pan over medium heat. Once hot, stir fry ginger for about 1 minute until aromatic. Pour in ketchup mixture.

3. When it simmers, lower heat to medium-low. Add sugar and honey. Cook for 1 minute, stirring frequently. Remove from heat. Set aside.

4. Preheat grill over high heat. Coat top with olive oil. Pat-dry the shrimp using a paper towel, then season all sides with salt and pepper.

5. Add to grill and cook for 1 to 2 minutes until color changes. Turn shrimp, then coat cooked side with prepared glaze mixture.

6. Grill until the bottom side is cooked, then turn again. Apply the glaze to the side. Remove from grill. Serve.

Nutrition:

Calories 199

Fat 5 g

Carbs 14 g

Sugar 8 g

Protein 24 g

Sodium 750 mg

26. DIY Red Hook's Lobster Pound

Preparation time: 10 minutes

Cooking time: 10 minutes

Servings: 2

Ingredients:

- 2 large egg yolks
- 1 teaspoon Dijon mustard
- 4 teaspoons fresh lemon juice, plus more
- 1 cup of vegetable oil
- Coarse salt and ground pepper, to taste
- ¾ pounds lobster meat, cooked and chopped into 1-inch cubes
- 2 top-split hot dog rolls
- 2 tablespoons butter, melted
- Iceberg lettuce, shredded
- 1 scallion, finely sliced
- Paprika, to taste

Directions:

1. To make the DIY mayonnaise, add egg yolks, mustard, and lemon juice to a food processor. Process until thoroughly mixed.

2. Then, while still processing, gradually add oil until the mixture thickens and becomes cloudy. Add salt and pepper.

3. Transfer to a bowl and cover. Set aside.

4. Prepare lobster filling by combining lobster pieces, prepared mayonnaise, lemon juice, salt, and pepper in a bowl.

5. Heat griddle. Apply butter to insides of hotdog rolls. Place rolls to grill butter side down, and cook until golden brown.

6. Assemble lobster rolls by layering lettuce, lobster and mayonnaise mixture, scallions, and paprika. Repeat for 2nd lobster roll. Serve.

Nutrition:

Calories 1746

Fat 135 g

Carbs 49 g

Sugar 9 g

Fibers 5 g

Protein 92 g

Sodium 2299 mg

27. Copycat Bubba Gum's Coconut Shrimp

Preparation time: 5 minutes

Cooking time: 20 minutes

Servings: 2

Ingredients:

- Oil, for deep frying
- ½ pound medium raw shrimp, peeled and deveined
- ¾ cup pancake mix
- ¼ teaspoon cayenne pepper
- 1 cup shredded coconut
- ¾ cup wheat beer
- ¼ cup all-purpose flour
- ¼ teaspoon seasoning salt
- ¼ teaspoon garlic powder

Sauce:

- ¼ cup orange marmalade
- ½ teaspoon Cajun seasoning

Directions:

1. Preheat deep fryer to 350°F.
2. Run cold water over shrimp, then dry using a paper towel. Set aside.
3. Prepare 3 bowls for the different coatings. In the 1st bowl, combine pancake mix and beer. In the 2nd, combine flour, seasoning salt, cayenne pepper, and garlic powder. For the 3rd bowl, add coconut.
4. One at a time, dredge shrimp into 1st bowl, shaking excess flour, then into the 2nd bowl followed by the 3rd.
5. Deep fry shrimp for about 45 to 60 seconds until lightly brown. Then, transfer onto a plate lined with paper towels to drain.
6. For the sauce, mix the sauce fixing in a bowl. Serve.

Nutrition:

calories 609

fat 15 g

carbs 84 g

sugar 35 g

fibers 6 g

protein 32 g

28. Tony Roma's Grilled Salmon with Carolina Honeys Sauce

Preparation time: 5 minutes

Cooking time: 60 minutes

Servings: 4

Ingredients:

- 1 cup ketchup
- 1 cup apple cider vinegar
- ½ cup molasses
- ½ cup honey
- 1 teaspoon hickory liquid smoke
- 1½ teaspoons salt, divided
- ½ teaspoon garlic powder, divided
- ¼ teaspoon onion powder
- ¼ teaspoon Tabasco pepper sauce
- ½ teaspoon ground black pepper
- ¼ teaspoon paprika
- ¼ teaspoon ground cayenne pepper
- 4 6-ounce skinless salmon fillets
- Olive oil cooking spray or olive oil

Directions:

1. To make the sauce, add ketchup, vinegar, molasses, honey, liquid smoke, ½ teaspoon salt, ¼ teaspoon garlic powder, onion powder, and Tabasco sauce to a deep pan.

2. Heat over medium-high heat, stirring to mix until smooth. Bring to a boil, then reduce heat. Let simmer within 30 minutes until the mixture becomes thick.

3. Spray or brush grill with olive oil. Preheat grill to high heat.

4. Prepare dry seasoning by mixing remaining salt and garlic powder, black pepper, paprika, and cayenne pepper in a bowl.

5. Rub salmon with seasoning mixture on all sides. Add salmon to grill and cook for 3 minutes. Rotate to 180 degrees to create crisscross marks, then turn.

6. Repeat process with the other side. Remove from grill once fillets are cooked through.

7. Transfer to a serving plate. Serve with sauce drizzled on top.

Nutrition:

calories 579

fat 10 g

carbs 86 g

sugar 58 g

fibers 0 g

protein 36 g

29. Red Lobster's Cajun Shrimp

Preparation time: 10 minutes

Cooking time: 15 minutes

Servings: 4

Ingredients:

- ½ cup butter, melted
- 1-pound medium shrimp, peeled and deveined
- 4 teaspoons cayenne pepper
- 3 teaspoons salt
- 2 teaspoons black pepper
- 2 teaspoons paprika
- Lemon wedges
- 2 teaspoons cumin
- 2¼ teaspoons dry mustard
- 1 teaspoon dried thyme
- 1 teaspoon dried oregano
- 2 teaspoons onion powder
- 2 teaspoons garlic powder

Directions:

1. Preheat oven to 400°F.
2. Coat the bottom of a baking tray using a butter. Arrange shrimp onto the tray.
3. Combine remaining ingredients in a bowl and rub onto shrimp to season. Make sure shrimp are thoroughly and evenly coated with both butter and seasoning mixture.
4. Place in oven and bake for about 10 to 15 minutes until color changes.
5. Serve with lemon wedges on the side.

Nutrition:

Calories 341

Fat 25 g

Carbs 5 g

Sugar 1 g

Fibers 2 g

Protein 25 g

30. "Applebee's" Honey Grilled Salmon

Preparation time: 15 minutes

Cooking time: 23 minutes

Servings: 4

Ingredients:

- 4 teaspoons olive oil, divided
- ¼ cup dark brown sugar, packed
- ¼ cup pineapple juice
- 2 tablespoons fresh lemon juice
- 2 tablespoons white distilled vinegar
- ½ teaspoon paprika
- ½ teaspoon cayenne pepper
- ¼ teaspoon garlic powder
- Salt and ground black pepper, as required
- 4 salmon fillets

Directions:

1. In a saucepan, add 2 teaspoons of oil and remaining ingredients except for salmon fillets over medium-low heat and boil, stirring occasionally.
2. Adjust to low, then simmer, uncovered for about 15 minutes, stirring occasionally.
3. Preheat the barbecue grill to medium heat. Grease the grill grate. Rub the salmon fillets with remaining olive oil and sprinkle with salt and pepper.
4. Place the salmon fillets onto the grill and cook for about 3-4 minutes per side.

5. Remove the salmon fillets from the grill and brush each fillet with the honey sauce. Serve hot.

Nutrition:

Calories: 276

Fat: 13.6g

Protein: 27.7g

Carbs: 11.5g

Fiber: 0.2g

Sugar: 10.6g

31. "Long Johns Silver's" Batter-Dipped Fish

Preparation time: 15 minutes

Cooking time: 6 minutes

Servings: 6

Ingredients:

- 2 cups flour
- ¼ cup cornstarch
- 2 teaspoons sugar
- ½ teaspoon baking soda
- ½ teaspoon baking powder
- ½ teaspoon paprika
- ½ teaspoon onion salt

- Salt and ground black pepper, as required
- 16 ounces club soda
- 2 pounds cod, cut into 3-ounce slices
- 2-3 cups vegetable oil

Directions:

1. In a large bowl, add flour, cornstarch, sugar, baking soda, baking powder, paprika, onion salt, salt, and black pepper and mix well.
2. Put the club soda and mix until well combined. Coat the fish slices with flour mixture evenly.
3. Warm-up the oil in a large skillet and fry the fish slices for about 2-3 minutes or until golden brown.
4. Transfer the fish slices onto a paper towel-lined plate to drain. Serve warm.

Nutrition:

Calories: 942

Fat: 74.5g

Protein: 38.9g

Carbs: 38.3g

Fiber: 1.3g

Sugar: 1.5g

32. "Popeye's" Cajun Fish

Preparation time: 15 minutes

Cooking time: 8 minutes

Servings: 4

Ingredients:

- 2 pounds boneless, skinless catfish fillets, cut into 2-inch strips
- 1 cup buttermilk
- 1 large egg
- ¼ cup flour
- ¼ cup corn muffin mix
- 1 teaspoon Louisiana hot sauce
- 1 teaspoon dried oregano
- 1 teaspoon dried thyme
- 2 teaspoons ground mustard
- 2½ teaspoons paprika
- 2 teaspoons garlic powder
- 1 teaspoon onion powder
- 1 teaspoon cayenne pepper
- 2 teaspoons ground black pepper
- Salt, as required
- ½ cup of vegetable oil

Directions:

1. In a large bowl, soak the fish strips in buttermilk for about 30-45 minutes.
2. In a separate bowl, add egg, flour, and corn mix and beat until smooth.
3. Add the hot sauce, herbs, mustard, and spices and stir to combine.
4. Refrigerate the mixture for about 10-15 minutes.
5. Remove the fish strips from buttermilk and then coat with flour mixture evenly.
6. Warm-up the oil over medium-high heat in a large skillet and fry fish strips for about 3-4 minutes per side.
7. With a slotted spoon, transfer the fish strips onto a paper towel-lined plate to drain. Serve warm.

Nutrition:

Calories: 692

Fat: 48.8g

Protein: 41.9g

Carbs: 22.2g

Fiber: 3.5g

Sugar: 6.1g

33. "Bonefish Grill" Pan-Fried Tilapia with Chimichurri Sauce

Preparation time: 15 minutes

Cooking time: 8 minutes

Servings: 4

Ingredients:

For Tilapia:

- 4 tilapia fillets
- 2 tablespoons BBQ seasoning
- Salt and ground black pepper, as required
- 2 teaspoons olive oil

For Chimichurri Sauce:

- 8 garlic cloves, minced
- Salt, as required
- 1 teaspoon dried oregano
- 1 teaspoon ground black pepper
- 1 teaspoon red pepper flakes, crushed
- 4-5 teaspoons lemon zest, grated finely
- 4 ounces fresh lemon juice
- 1 bunch fresh flat-leaf parsley
- 1 cup olive oil

Directions:

1. For Chimichurri sauce: in a food processor, add all ingredients and pulse until well combined.
2. Transfer the sauce into a bowl and refrigerate to marinate for 30 minutes before serving.
3. Meanwhile, for tilapia: season each tilapia fillet with BBQ seasoning, salt, and black pepper.
4. Warm-up oil over medium-high heat in a non-stick pan and cook the tilapia fillets for about 3-4 minutes on each side.
5. Divide tilapia fillets onto serving plates.
6. Top each fillet with Chimichurri sauce and serve.

Nutrition:

Calories: 570

Fat: 52.1g

Protein: 27.2g

Carbs: 3.9g

Fiber: 0.8g

Sugar: 0.9g

34. Luby's Baked Fish

Preparation time: 15 minutes

Cooking time: 20 minutes

Servings: 6

Ingredients:

- 1 cup flour
- 1 cup buttermilk
- 3 eggs
- ½ teaspoon salt
- ¼ teaspoon ground black pepper
- 2 1/3 cups saltine crackers, crushed
- 6 haddock fillets

Directions:

1. Warm the oven to 350 degrees F. Line a large baking sheet with parchment paper.
2. Place flour in a large bowl, then in a second bowl, add buttermilk, eggs, salt, and black pepper and beat until well combined. In a third bowl, place crushed crackers.
3. Cover the fish fillets with the flour, then dip into the buttermilk mixture and finally coat with crackers. Arrange the coated fish fillets onto the prepared baking sheet in a single layer.
4. Bake within 20 minutes or until fish is done completely. Serve hot.

Nutrition:

Calories: 358

Fat: 6.1g

Protein: 42.3g

Carbs: 30.5g

Fiber: 1.1g

Sugar: 2.3g

35. "Ruth Chris Steakhouse" Shrimp Orleans

Preparation time: 15 minutes

Cooking time: 10 minutes

Servings: 4

Ingredients:

- ½ pound butter softened
- 2 tablespoons garlic, chopped
- ¼ teaspoon dried rosemary, crushed
- 1 teaspoon Worcestershire sauce
- ½ teaspoon Tabasco sauce
- 1 teaspoon ground black pepper
- ¾ teaspoon paprika

- 1/8 teaspoon cayenne pepper
- ½ teaspoon salt
- ¾ teaspoon water
- 1 tablespoon plus 1 teaspoon olive oil
- 1-pound shrimp, peeled and deveined
- ¼ cup scallions, chopped
- ½ cup dry white wine
- 4 sourdough bread slices

Directions:

1. For barbecue butter: In a bowl, add butter, garlic, rosemary, Worcestershire sauce, Tabasco sauce, black pepper, paprika, cayenne pepper, salt, and water, and with an electric mixer, beat on high speed until well combined. Refrigerate until serving.

2. Warm-up oil over medium-high heat in a large saucepan and cook the shrimp for about 1-2 minutes.

3. Adjust the heat to medium and flip the shrimp. Add scallions and cook for about 1-2 minutes.

4. Put the white wine and cook until reduced to ¼ cup. Add 1 cup of barbecue butter and stir to combine.

5. Adjust to low and cook for about 1-2 minutes, stirring frequently.

6. Remove from the heat and transfer into a warm bowl. Serve immediately.

Nutrition:

Calories: 632

Fat: 51.8g

Protein: 27.5g

Carbs: 9.8g

Fiber: 0.8g

Sugar: 1.1g

36. "Panda Express" Honey Walnut Shrimp

Preparation time: 15 minutes

Cooking time: 10 minutes

Servings: 4

Ingredients:

- 1 cup of water
- 2/3 cup white sugar
- ½ cup walnut halves
- 4 egg whites
- 2/3 cup cornstarch
- 1-pound large shrimp, peeled and deveined
- ¼ cup mayonnaise

- 2 tablespoons honey
- 1 tablespoon sweetened condensed milk
- 1 cup of vegetable oil

Directions:

1. Put the water, sugar, and walnuts in a small saucepan and boil. Cook for about 2 minutes.
2. Remove the walnuts from heat and place on a dish to dry.
3. In a bowl, add the egg whites and beat until foamy. Add the cornstarch and beat until well combined.
4. Coat the shrimp with cornstarch mixture evenly and let them drip off excess.
5. Warm-up the oil over medium-high heat in a medium pan and fry for about 4-5 minutes until light golden brown.
6. For the sauce: in a bowl, add the mayonnaise, honey, and condensed milk and beat until well combined.
7. Add the fried shrimp into the bowl of sauce and gently stir to combine.
8. Divide the shrimp onto serving plates and serve with the topping of candied walnuts.

Nutrition:

Calories: 680

Fat: 30.2g

Protein: 33.8g

Carbs: 71.1g

Fiber: 1.3g

Sugar: 45.9g

Chapter 5. Poultry

37. Cracker Barrel's Chicken Fried Chicken

Preparation Time: 15 minutes

Cooking Time: 30 minutes

Servings: 4

Ingredients:

Chicken:

- ½ cup all-purpose flour
- 1 teaspoon poultry seasoning
- ½ teaspoon salt
- ½ teaspoon pepper
- 1 egg, slightly beaten
- 1 tablespoon water
- 4 chicken breasts, pounded to a ½-inch thickness
- 1 cup of vegetable oil

Gravy:

- 2 tablespoons all-purpose flour
- ¼ teaspoon salt
- ¼ teaspoon pepper
- 1¼ cups milk

Directions:

1. Preheat the oven to 200°F. Mix the poultry seasoning, flour, salt, and pepper.
2. In another shallow dish, mix the beaten egg and water.
3. Cover the chicken breasts with the flour mixture, then dip them in the egg mixture. After this, coat it back into the flour mixture.
4. Warm-up the vegetable oil over medium-high heat in a large deep skillet. Put the chicken and cook for 15 minutes, or until fully cooked, turning over about halfway through.
5. Put the chicken on a baking sheet, then place in the oven to maintain temperature.
6. Remove all but 2 tablespoons of oil from the skillet you cooked the chicken in.
7. Prepare the gravy by whisking the dry gravy ingredients together in a bowl. Then whisk them into the oil in the skillet, stirring thoroughly to remove lumps.
8. When the flour begins to brown, slowly whisk in the milk for about 2 minutes or until the mixture thickens.
9. Top chicken with some of the gravy.

Nutrition:

Calories: 242.8

Fat: 6.6g

Carbs: 38.4g

Sugars: 3g

Protein: 8.4g

38. Cracker Barrel's Broccoli Cheddar Chicken

Preparation Time: 10 minutes

Cooking Time: 45 minutes

Servings: 4

Ingredients:

- 4 skinless chicken breasts
- 1 cup milk
- 1 cup Ritz-style crackers, crushed
- 1 can condensed cheddar cheese soup
- ½ pound frozen broccoli
- 6 ounces cheddar cheese, shredded
- ½ teaspoon salt
- ½ teaspoon pepper

Directions:

1. Preheat the oven to 350°F. Whisk the milk and cheddar cheese soup together in a mixing bowl.

2. Prepare a baking dish by greasing the sides, then lay the chicken in the bottom and season with the salt and pepper.

3. Put the soup mixture on the chicken, then top with the crackers, broccoli, and shredded cheese—Bake for 45 minutes.

Nutrition:

Calories: 150

Fat: 4.2g

Carbs: 40g

Sugars: 1g

Protein: 9g

39. Cracker Barrel's Grilled Chicken Tenderloin

Preparation Time: 10 minutes

Cooking Time: 30 minutes

Servings: 4–5

Ingredients:

- 4–5 boneless and skinless chicken breasts, cut into strips
- 1 cup Italian dressing
- 2 teaspoons lime juice
- 4 teaspoons honey

Directions:

1. Mix the honey, sauce, and lime juice in a plastic bag. Seal and shake to combine.

2. Place the chicken in the bag. Seal and shake again, then transfer to the refrigerator for at least 1 hour.

3. When ready to prepare, transfer the chicken and the marinade to a large nonstick skillet.

4. Let it boil and allow it to simmer until the liquid has cooked down to a glaze.

Nutrition:

Calories: 100

Fat: 3g

Carbs: 21g

Sugars: 10g

Protein: 5g

40. Cracker Barrel's Sunday Chicken

Preparation Time: 10 minutes

Cooking Time: 10 minutes

Servings: 4

Ingredients:

- Oil for frying
- 4 boneless, skinless chicken breasts
- 1 cup all-purpose flour
- 1 cup bread crumbs
- 2 teaspoons salt
- 2 teaspoons black pepper
- 1 cup buttermilk
- ½ cup of water

Directions:

1. Add 3–4 inches of oil to a large pot or a deep fryer and preheat to 350°F.

2. Mix the flour, breadcrumbs, salt, and pepper in a shallow dish. To a separate shallow dish, add the buttermilk and water; stir.

3. Pound the chicken breasts to a consistent size. Let it dry paper towel and season with salt and pepper.

4. Dip the seasoned breasts in the flour mixture, then the buttermilk mixture, then back into the flour.

5. Put the breaded chicken in the pan and fry for about 8 minutes. Turn the chicken as necessary so that it cooks evenly on both sides.

6. Remove the chicken to either a wire rack or a plate lined with paper towels to drain.

7. Serve with mashed potatoes.

Nutrition:

Calories: 150

Fat: 20g

Carbs: 50g

Sugars: 9g

Protein: 15g

41. Cracker Barrel's Creamy Chicken and Rice

Preparation Time: 10 minutes

Cooking Time: 45 minutes

Servings: 4

Ingredients:

- Salt and pepper to taste
- 2 cups cooked rice
- 1 diced onion
- 1 can cream of mushroom soup
- 1 packet chicken gravy
- 1½ pounds chicken breasts, cut into strips

Directions:

1. Preheat the oven to 350°F.

2. Cook the rice. When it is just about finished, toss in the diced onion so that it cooks too.

3. Spray the baking dish with some nonstick cooking spray.

4. Dump the rice into the prepared baking dish, then layer the chicken strips on top. Pour the cream of mushroom soup on the chicken.

5. Whisk the chicken gravy with 1 cup water, making sure to get all the lumps out. Put the mixture over the casserole.

6. Cover it with foil, then bake for 45 minutes or until the chicken is thoroughly cooked.

Nutrition:

Calories: 160

Fat: 10g

Carbs: 50g

Sugars: 6g

Protein: 12g

42. Cracker Barrel's Campfire Chicken

Preparation Time: 10 minutes

Cooking Time: 45 minutes

Servings: 4

Ingredients:

- 1 tablespoon paprika
- 2 teaspoons onion powder
- 2 teaspoons salt
- 1 teaspoon garlic powder
- 1 teaspoon dried rosemary
- 1 teaspoon black pepper
- 1 teaspoon dried oregano
- 1 whole chicken, quartered
- 2 carrots, cut into thirds
- 3 red skin potatoes, halved
- 1 ear of corn, quartered
- 1 tablespoon olive oil
- 1 tablespoon butter
- 5 sprigs fresh thyme

Directions:

1. Preheat the oven to 400°F.
2. Mix the paprika, onion powder, salt, garlic powder, rosemary, pepper, and oregano.
3. Add the chicken quarters and 1 tablespoon of the spice mix to a large plastic freezer bag. Cover and put inside the refrigerator for at least 1 hour.

4. Put the carrots, corn, and potatoes in a bowl. Put some olive oil and the rest of the spice mix. Toss to coat.

5. Preheat a large skillet over high heat. Add some oil, and when it is hot, add the chicken pieces and cook until golden brown.

6. Prepare 4 pieces of aluminum foil and add some carrots, potatoes, corn, and a chicken quarter to each. Top with some butter and thyme.

7. Fold the foil in and make pouches by sealing the edges tightly—Bake for 45 minutes.

Nutrition:

Calories: 140

Fat: 8g

Carbs: 30

Sugars: 10g

Protein: 25g

43. Cracker Barrel's Chicken and Dumplings

Preparation Time: 30 minutes

Cooking Time: 20 minutes

Servings: 4

Ingredients:

- 2 cups flour
- ½ teaspoon baking powder
- 1 pinch salt
- 2 tablespoons butter
- 1 scant cup buttermilk
- 2 quarts chicken broth
- 3 cups cooked chicken

Directions:

1. Mix in a bowl the salt, flour, and baking powder in a large bowl to make the dumplings. Cut the butter into the flour mixture. Put in the milk until it forms a dough ball.
2. Put enough flour on your working station. Roll out your dough relatively thin, then cut into squares to form dumplings.
3. Flour a plate and transfer the dough from the counter to the plate.
4. Bring the chicken broth to a boil in a large saucepan, then drop the dumplings in one by one, stirring continually.
5. The excess flour will thicken the broth. Cook it for 20-25 minutes or until the dumplings are no longer doughy.
6. Add the chicken, stir to combine, and serve.

Nutrition:

Calories: 115

Fat: 14g

Carbs: 78g

Sugars: 9g

Protein: 8g

44. Red Lobster's Classic BBQ Chicken

Preparation time: 5 minutes

Cooking time: 1 hour 45 minutes

Servings: 4–6

Ingredients:

- 4 pounds of chicken
- Salt
- Olive oil
- 1 cup barbecue sauce

Directions:

1. Put some olive oil and salt all over the chicken. In the meanwhile, preheat the griddle with high heat.
2. Grill the chicken skin side for 10 minutes. Cover the chicken with foil and grill for 30 minutes in low heat.
3. Put some barbecue sauce all over the chicken. Cook the chicken for another 20 minutes.
4. Baste, cover, and cook again for 30 minutes.

5. Baste with more barbecue sauce to serve!

Nutrition:

Calories: 539

Fat: 11.6g

Carbs: 15.1g

Sugar: 0.3g

Protein: 87.6g

45. Chipotle's Grilled Sweet Chili Lime Chicken

Preparation time: 35 minutes

Cooking time: 15 minutes

Servings: 4

Ingredients:

- ½ cup sweet chili sauce
- ¼ cup of soy sauce
- 1 teaspoon marina juice
- 1 teaspoon orange juice, fresh squeezed
- 1 teaspoon orange marmalade
- 2 tablespoons lime juice
- 1 tablespoon brown sugar
- 1 clove garlic, minced

- 4 boneless, skinless chicken breasts
- Sesame seeds, for garnish

Directions:

1. Whisk sweet chili sauce, soy sauce, marina, orange marmalade, lime and orange juice, brown sugar, and the minced garlic together in a small mixing bowl.

2. Set aside ¼ cup of the sauce. Coat the chicken in sauce to coat and let it marinate 30 minutes.

3. Preheat your griddle to medium heat. Cook each side of the chicken on the grill for 7 minutes.

4. Baste the cooked chicken with remaining marinade and garnish with sesame seeds to serve with your favorite sides.

Nutrition:

Calories: 380

Sugar: 0.5g

Fat: 12g

Carbs: 19.7g

Protein: 43.8g

46. Chipotle's Adobo Chicken

Preparation time: 1 –24 hours

Cooking time: 20 minutes

Servings: 4 – 6

Ingredients:

- 2 lbs. chicken thighs or breasts (boneless, skinless)

For the marinade:

- ¼ cup olive oil
- 2 chipotle peppers
- 1 teaspoon adobo sauce
- 1 tablespoon garlic, minced
- 1 shallot, finely chopped

- 1 ½ tablespoons cumin
- 1 tablespoon cilantro, super-finely chopped or dried
- 2 teaspoons chili powder
- 1 teaspoon dried oregano
- ½ teaspoon salt
- Fresh limes, garnish
- Cilantro, garnish

Directions:

1. Preheat grill to medium-high. Blend the marinade ingredients to turn it into a paste.
2. Add the chicken and marinade to a sealable plastic bag and massage to coat well.
3. Put in the fridge before grilling. Grill the chicken for 7 minutes, turn and grill an additional 7 minutes; or until good grill marks appear.
4. Continue to grill in low heat until chicken is cooked through, and the internal temperature reaches 165°F.
5. After that, remove it from the grill and allow to rest 5 to 10 minutes before serving.
6. Squeeze fresh lime and sprinkle cilantro to serve.

Nutrition:

Calories: 561

Sugar: 0.3g

Fat: 23.8g

Carbs: 18.7g

47. Chipotle's Classic Grilled Chicken

Preparation time: 8 – 24 hours

Cooking time: 20 minutes

Servings: 4

Ingredients:

- 2 lbs. boneless, skinless chicken thighs

For the marinade:

- ¼ cup fresh lime juice
- 2 teaspoon lime zest
- ¼ cup honey
- 2 tablespoons olive oil
- 1 tablespoon balsamic vinegar
- ½ teaspoon of sea salt
- ½ teaspoon black pepper
- 2 garlic cloves, minced
- ¼ teaspoon onion powder

Directions:

1. Mix the marinade fixings in a large bowl; reserve 2 tablespoons of the marinade for grilling.
2. Add chicken and marinade to a sealable plastic bag and marinate 8 hours or overnight in the refrigerator.
3. Preheat grill to medium heat and brush lightly with olive oil. Put the chicken on the grill and cook 8 minutes per side.
4. Coat the chicken in the marinade in the last few minutes of cooking until it reaches the internal temperature of 165°F.
5. Place the chicken, tent with foil, and allow resting for 5 minutes. Serve and enjoy!

Nutrition:

Calories: 381

Sugar: 1.1g

Fat: 20.2g

Carbs: 4.7g

Protein: 44.7g

48. Panda Express' Orange Chicken

Preparation Time: 15 minutes

Cooking Time: 30 minutes

Servings: 6

Ingredients:

Orange sauce:

- 1½ tablespoon soy sauce
- 1½ tablespoon water
- 5 tablespoons sugar
- 5 tablespoons white vinegar
- 3 tablespoons orange zest

Chicken preparation:

- 1 egg
- 1½ teaspoon salt
- White pepper, to taste
- 5 tablespoons grapeseed oil, divided
- ½ cup + 1 tablespoon cornstarch
- ¼ cup flour
- ¼ cup of cold water
- 2 pounds chicken breast, chopped
- 1 teaspoon fresh ginger, grated
- 1 teaspoon garlic, finely chopped
- ½ teaspoon hot red chili pepper, ground
- ¼ cup green onion, sliced
- 1 tablespoon rice wine

- ½ teaspoon sesame oil
- White rice and steamed broccoli for serving

Directions:

1. Mix ingredients for the orange sauce in a bowl. Reserve for future use

2. Add egg, salt, pepper, and 1 tablespoon oil to a separate bowl. Mix well.

3. In another bowl, combine ½ cup cornstarch and flour. Mix until thoroughly blended.

4. Add remaining cornstarch and cold water in a different bowl. Blend until cornstarch is completely dissolved.

5. Warm-up 3 tablespoons oil in a large deep skillet or wok over high heat.

6. Coat chicken pieces in the egg mixture. Let excess drip off. Then, coat in cornstarch mixture.

7. Cook within 3 minutes or until both sides are golden brown and chicken is cooked through, then pat-dry.

8. In a clean large deep skillet or wok, heat the remaining oil on high heat. Lightly sauté ginger and garlic for 30 seconds or until aromatic.

9. Toss in peppers and green onions. Stir-fry vegetables for 1-3 minutes, then pour in rice wine. Mix well before adding the orange sauce. Bring to a boil.

10. Mix in cooked chicken pieces, then adds cornstarch mixture. Simmer until mixture is thick, then mix in sesame oil.

11. Transfer onto a plate and serve with white rice and steamed broccoli.

Nutrition:

Calories 305

Fat 5 g

Carbs 27 g

Protein 34 g

Sodium 1024 mg

49. Chick-fil-A Chicken Nuggets with Honey Mustard Dip

Preparation Time: 15 minutes

Cooking Time: 20 minutes

Servings: 2

Ingredients:

- 1 egg
- ¾ cup milk
- ¼ cup dill pickle juice
- 2 large chicken breasts, bite-sized
- Salt and pepper to taste
- 1¼ cups all-purpose flour
- 2 tablespoons powdered sugar
- 2 teaspoons salt
- 1 teaspoon pepper
- ½ cup canola oil
- ½ cup plain Greek yogurt
- 1½ tablespoons yellow mustard
- 1 tablespoon Dijon mustard
- 2 tablespoons honey

Directions:

1. Mix egg, milk, and pickle juice in a bowl until well combined. Season chicken pieces with salt and pepper and then add to egg mixture. Put in the refrigerator within 2 hours to marinate.

2. In another bowl, add flour, powdered sugar, salt, and pepper. Mix well until combined—transfer chicken from the marinade into the flour mixture. Toss and fold to coat thoroughly and evenly on all sides.

3. Heat ½ cup oil in a large pan over medium-high heat.

4. One at a time, slowly adds chicken into the hot oil. Allow spacing between pieces. In-depth fry pieces for about 3 to 4 minutes until one side is lightly brown.

5. Using tongs, turn slices over and continue cooking for another 3 to 4 minutes. Move it to a plate lined with paper towels.

6. For the dipping sauce, combine Greek yogurt, both mustards, and honey in a bowl. Mix well. Serve on the side with hot chicken pieces.

Nutrition:

Calories 395

Fat 6 g

Carbs 45 g

Sugar 16 g

Fibers 2 g

Protein 39 g

Sodium 1434 mg

50. Boneless Buffalo Wings

Preparation Time: 10 minutes

Cooking Time: 15 minutes

Servings: 2

Ingredients:

- 2 chicken breasts
- 4 to 6 cups vegetable oil

Batter:

- 1 cup flour
- 2 teaspoons salt
- ½ teaspoon black pepper
- ¼ teaspoon cayenne pepper
- ¼ teaspoon paprika
- 1 egg
- 1 cup milk

Buffalo Sauce:

- ¼ cup hot sauce or to taste
- 1 tablespoon margarine

Directions:

1. For the batter, mix the flour, salt, peppers, and paprika in a medium bowl. Mix the egg plus milk in a separate bowl.

2. For the chicken, slice the chicken breast into small pieces. Put the chicken into the egg mixture first, then into the batter. Repeat until each piece of the chicken is coated twice.

3. Refrigerate the breaded chicken for 10–20 minutes, so the batter has a chance to adhere to the chicken.

4. Heat enough oil in a pot to cook the chicken. It should be 350°F.

5. Drop a few chicken pieces at a time into the hot oil—Cook within 5 minutes, or until nicely browned.

6. Dissolve the butter over medium heat in a small saucepan and stir in the hot sauce. Toss the chicken pieces in hot sauce to coat.

Nutrition:

Calories: 1170

Fat: 70g

Carbs: 67g

Protein: 71g

Fiber: 8g

51. Chicken Quesadilla

Preparation Time: 5 minutes

Cooking Time: 10 minutes

Servings: 2

Ingredients:

- 2 (12 inches) flour tortillas
- 1 tablespoon butter, melted
- 2 tablespoons chipotle pepper sauce (optional)
- 4 ounces grilled chicken (spicy seasoning optional)
- ¼ cup pepper jack cheese, shredded
- ¼ cup tomato, diced

Optional toppings:

- Jalapeño pepper, diced
- Onion, diced
- Cilantro, minced
- Bacon, fried and crumbled
- 1 cup lettuce, shredded

To serve:

- Sour cream
- Green onion
- Salsa

Directions:

1. Preheat a large skillet over medium heat.

2. Drizzle one side of each tortilla with melted butter. Place one tortilla butter side down on your counter or cutting board.

3. Top the tortilla with chipotle sauce, then sprinkle on the grilled chicken. Add the cheese, tomato, and other desired toppings; repeat it on the other tortilla, butter side up, and transfer it to the skillet.

4. Cook each side within 3 minutes (or until the tortilla starts to crisp up), then flip and cook on the other hand, making sure the cheese has melted completely, but not so long that the lettuce (if used) is wilted.

5. Serve the quesadilla with sour cream, green onion, and salsa.

Nutrition:

Calories: 800

Fat: 43.8g

Carbs: 52.9g

Protein: 44.9g

Fiber: 10g

52. Pei Wei's Sesame Chicken

Preparation Time: 20 minutes

Cooking Time: 15 minutes

Servings: 2

Ingredients:

Sauce:

- ½ cup of soy sauce
- 2½ tablespoons hoisin sauce
- ½ cup of sugar
- ¼ cup white vinegar
- 2½ tablespoons of rice wine
- 2½ tablespoons chicken broth
- Pinch of white pepper
- 1¼ tablespoons orange zest

Breaded chicken:

- 2 pounds boneless skinless chicken breasts
- ¼ cup cornstarch
- ½ cup flour
- 1 egg
- 2 cups of milk
- Pinch of white pepper
- Pinch of salt
- 1-quart vegetable oil
- ½ red bell pepper, chunked
- ½ white onion, chunked
- 1 tablespoon Asian chili sauce

- ½ tablespoon ginger, minced
- ¼ cup scallions, white part only, cut into rings
- 1 tablespoon sesame oil
- 1 tablespoon cornstarch
- 1 tablespoon water
- Sesame seeds for garnish

Directions:

1. For the sauce, mix all the sauce fixings in a small saucepan. Simmer, then remove from the heat and set aside.

2. Mix the eggs, milk, salt, plus pepper in a shallow dish.

3. Mix the ¼ cup of cornstarch and flour in a separate shallow dish.

4. Put the chicken in the egg batter, then in the cornstarch/flour mixture. Shake off any excess, then set aside.

5. Warm-up the vegetable oil on medium-high heat in a deep skillet or saucepan.

6. When hot, drop the coated chicken into the oil and cook for about 2–4 minutes. Remove from oil and place on a paper-towel-lined plate to drain.

7. Make a slurry out of the 1 tablespoon of cornstarch and water.

8. In a different large skillet or wok, heat 1 tablespoon of sesame oil until hot. Add the ginger and chili sauce and heat for about 10 seconds.

9. Put the peppers plus onions, then cook for another 30 seconds. Stir in the chili sauce and ginger and the sauce you made earlier and boil.

10. Once it boils, stir in the cornstarch slurry and cook until the sauce thickens.

11. Put the chicken when the sauce is thick and stir to coat. Serve it with rice, then sprinkle with sesame seeds.

Nutrition:

Calories: 293

Fat: 14g

Carbs: 27g

Protein: 14g

Fiber: 0.7g

53. Pei Wei's Coconut Curry with Chicken

Preparation Time: 15 minutes

Cooking Time: 30 minutes

Servings: 2

Ingredients:

- Meat from one whole chicken, or 6–8 chicken tenderloins, cooked
- 1 cup snow pea pods
- 2 red bell peppers, chopped
- 1 yellow or white onion, chopped
- 3 carrots, chopped
- 5 cloves garlic, minced
- 1-inch piece of ginger, minced
- 2 (14-ounce) cans of full-fat coconut milk
- ½ (2.8-ounce) pouch green curry paste
- One bunch Thai basil or regular basil, roughly chopped
- Salt and pepper to taste

Directions:

1. Mix the coconut milk plus green curry paste in a medium saucepan. Bring it to a simmer.
2. Add the cooked chicken and all of the vegetables. Continue to simmer until the vegetables are cooked through to your desired softness, about 15–20 minutes. Serve with rice.

Nutrition:

Calories: 320

Fat: 22g

Carbs: 8.5g

Protein: 25g

Fiber: 1.4g

Chapter 6. Meat

54. Southwest Steak

Preparation Time: 20 minutes

Cooking time: 10 minutes

Servings: 2

Ingredients:

- 2 (6-ounce) sirloin steaks, or your favorite cut
- 2 teaspoons blackened steak seasoning
- ½ cup red peppers, sliced

- ½ cup green peppers, sliced
- 2 tablespoons unsalted butter
- 1 cup yellow onion, sliced
- 2 cloves garlic, minced
- Salt, to taste
- Pepper, to taste
- 2 slices cheddar cheese
- 2 slices Monterey jack cheese
- Vegetable medley or/and garlic mashed potatoes, for serving

Directions:

1. Preheat a cast iron or a grill.
2. Season the meat with steak seasoning for about 3–4 minutes on each side for medium-rare.
3. In another skillet, melt the butter and cook the peppers, onion, and garlic—season with salt and pepper.
4. Before the steak was cooked, top with a slice of each cheese and cook until the cheese melts.
5. Serve the steaks with pepper and onion mix and garlic mashed potatoes.

Nutrition:

Calories:350

Fat: 17g

Carbs: 34g

Protein: 14g

Fiber: 2g

55. DIY Sizzling Steak, Cheese, and Mushrooms Skillet

Preparation Time: 15 minutes

Cooking Time: 1 hour 35 minutes

Servings: 4

Ingredients:

- 1 head garlic, cut crosswise
- 2 tablespoons olive oil, divided
- Salt and pepper, to taste
- 2 pounds Yukon Gold potatoes, chopped
- Water, for boiling
- 2 tablespoons butter
- 1 large yellow onion
- 8 ounces cremini mushrooms
- Salt and pepper to taste
- ½ cup milk
- ¼ cup cream

- 3 tablespoons butter
- 2½ pounds 1-inch thick sirloin steak, cut into 4 large pieces
- 8 slices mozzarella cheese

Directions:

1. Preheat oven to 300°F.
2. Position garlic on the foil. Pour 1 tablespoon olive oil to the garlic's cut, then cover a foil around the garlic.
3. Bake within 30 minutes, then remove and squeeze out the garlic from the head. Move it to a bowl, then put the salt plus pepper, then mash, and set aside.
4. Boil the potatoes in a pot; when it boils, adjust the heat to medium. Simmer within 20 to 25 minutes.
5. Dissolve the butter on a nonstick pan over medium-low heat. Add onions and sauté for about 15 minutes until a bit tender.
6. Toss in mushrooms and sauté, lower the heat to medium, then put salt plus pepper. Cook within 10 minutes more, then set aside.
7. Mash the drained potatoes with an electric mixer over low speed. Simultaneously, slowly put in the milk, cream, butter, plus the mashed garlic with olive oil.

8. Remove from the mixer and place a cover on top of the bowl. Set aside and keep warm.

9. Evenly coat steak pieces with remaining 1 tablespoon olive oil on all sides. Heat grill, then place the meat on the grill— Cook for 4 minutes.

10. Flip and add mozzarella slices on top. Cook again within 4 minutes.

11. Move the steaks to a serving plate, then top with onion or mushroom mixture. Place mashed potatoes on the side. Serve.

Nutrition:

Calories:270

Fat: 0g

Carbs:0g

Protein:22g

Fiber:0g

56. Outback Style Steak

Preparation Time: 40 minutes

Cooking time: 10 minutes

Servings: 4

Ingredients:

- 4 (6-ounce) sirloin or ribeye steaks
- 2 tablespoons olive oil
- 2 tablespoons Old Bay Seasoning
- 2 tablespoons brown sugar
- 1 teaspoon garlic powder
- 1 teaspoon salt
- ½ teaspoon black pepper
- ½ teaspoon onion powder
- ½ teaspoon ground cumin

Directions:

1. Let the steak sit within 20 minutes at room temperature.
2. Combine all the seasonings and mix well.
3. Rub the steaks with oil and some of the spice mixture, covering all the surfaces. Let the steaks sit for 20–30 minutes.
4. Meanwhile, heat your grill to medium-high.
5. Cook the steaks within 5 minutes on each side for medium-rare (or to an internal temperature of 130°F.) Allow sitting within 5 minutes before serving.

Nutrition:

Calories:254

Fat: 13g

Carbs:56g

Protein:45g

Fiber: 3g

57.Teriyaki Filet Medallions

Preparation Time: 15 minutes

Cooking time: 20 minutes

Servings: 4

Ingredients:

- 3 (6-ounce) sirloin or ribeye steaks
- 1 red bell pepper, squares
- 1 yellow bell pepper, squares
- 1 green pepper, cut into 1-inch squares
- 1 large red onion, outer layers cut into 1-inch squares

Teriyaki marinade:

- 1 cup of soy sauce
- ½ cup Apple Cider Vinegar
- ½ cup Sugar
- ½ cup Pineapple Juice

- 2 cloves garlic, minced
- 2 teaspoons fresh ginger, grated
- 1 teaspoon red pepper flakes

Directions:

1. Mix the marinade fixings in a mixing bowl.
2. Slice the steaks into 1-inch cubes, then place them in a resealable bag. Put aside a third of the marinade and pour the rest over the meat.
3. Seal and refrigerate for 4 hours or more, manipulating the bag from time to time.
4. Soak your skewers if they're wooden and heat the grill to medium. Thread the skewers by alternating meat and vegetables.
5. Grill within 5–10 minutes on each side, often brushing with the reserved marinade.

Nutrition:

Calories:681

Fat: 30g

Carbs:32g

Protein:71g

Fiber: 0g

58. Beef Stew

Preparation Time: 10 minutes

Cooking Time: 2 hours

Servings: 8

Ingredients:

- 1-pound stewing beef, in medium-sized chunks
- 3 tablespoons vegetable oil, divided
- Salt and pepper, to taste
- 1/2 cup flour1 onion, chopped
- 4 medium potatoes, cut into chunks

- 5 carrots, peeled and cut into chunks
- 1-quart beef broth
- 1/3 cup ketchup
- 1 cup peas

Directions:

1. Mix the flour, salt, plus pepper and toss with the meat.
2. Grease using a 2 tbsp of oil in a pot, then over medium-high heat brown beef in flour, add all the flour.
3. Stir often, so the flour and meat do not burn but brown nicely. Remove meat to a plate.
4. Add the last tablespoon of oil and sauté the onion until translucent, scraping up a browned bit from the meat.
5. Move the meat back to the pot, put the potatoes and carrots. Mix with the stock and ketchup.
6. Simmer on low heat, stirring within 1 1/2 hours. Adjust seasoning.
7. Add frozen peas just before serving. Stir to defrost and serve.

Nutrition:

Calories: 178

Carbohydrates: 17g

Protein: 16g

Fat: 4g

Cholesterol: 35mg

Sodium: 209mg

Fiber: 3g

Sugar: 3g

59. Meat Loaf

Preparation Time: 15 minutes

Cooking Time: 1 ½ hour

Servings: 6

Ingredients:

- 2 large eggs
- 2/3 cup whole milk
- 3 slices bread, torn
- 1/2 cup chopped onion
- 1/2 cup grated carrot
- 1 cup shredded cheddar
- 1 tablespoon parsley, minced
- 1 teaspoon dried basil
- 1 teaspoon salt
- 1/4 teaspoon pepper
- 1-1/2 pounds lean ground beef

Topping:

- 1/2 cup tomato sauce
- 1/2 cup packed brown sugar
- teaspoon prepared mustard

Directions:

1. Whisk the eggs in a bowl, then put the milk plus bread. Mix in the onion, carrot, cheese, plus the seasonings.
2. Put the beef over mixture, then shape into a 7-1/2x3-1/2x2-1/2 inches loaf in a shallow baking pan. Bake it uncovered, at 350° within 45 minutes.
3. Mix the topping fixings, spoon half of the batter over the meatloaf.
4. Bake within 30 minutes. Allow to cool down within 10 minutes before serving.

Nutrition:

Calories: 200

Carbs: 11g

Fat: 11g

Protein: 18g

60.   Roast Beef

Preparation Time: 20 minutes

Cooking Time: 2 ½ hours

Servings: 8

Ingredients:

- 1 tbsp canola oil
- 1 beef eye round roast
- 1 garlic clove, minced
- 2 tsp dried basil
- 1 tsp salt
- 1 tsp dried rosemary, crushed
-
- 1/2 tsp pepper
- 1 medium onion, chopped
- 1 teaspoon beef bouillon granules
- 1 cup brewed coffee
- 3/4 cup water

Gravy:

- 1/4 cup all-purpose flour
- 1/4 cup cold water

Directions:

1. Warm oil over medium heat in a Dutch oven; brown roast over all sides. Remove, then mix garlic plus seasonings, and sprinkle on the roast.

2. Put the onion into the same pan; cook on medium heat. Mix in the bouillon, coffee plus 3/4 cup water, then put the roast and boil.

3. Simmer, covered, within 2-1/2 hours, remove roast from pan, and set aside cooking juices. Cover it with foil, then let it cool down within 10 minutes.

4. Mix the flour plus cold water, then stir into cooking juices. Boil while stirring continuously—Cook and stir until thickened, 1-2 minutes. Serve with roast.

Nutrition:

Calories: 198

Fat: 6g

Cholesterol: 65mg

Sodium: 453mg

Carbohydrate: 5g

Protein: 28g

61. Grilled Pork Chops

Preparation Time: 20 minutes

Cooking Time: 10 minutes

Servings: 4

Ingredients:

- 1/4 cup kosher salt
- 1/4 cup sugar
- 2 cups of water
- 2 cups of ice water
- 4 center-cut pork rib chops
- 2 tablespoons canola oil

Basic Rub:

- 3 tablespoons paprika
- 1 teaspoon each:
- garlic powder
- onion powder
- ground cumin
- ground mustard
- 1 teaspoon coarsely ground pepper
- 1/2 teaspoon ground chipotle pepper

Directions:

1. Mix the salt, sugar, and 2 cups water in a large saucepan; cook on medium heat, then remove.

2. Put 2 cups ice water to cool brine at room temperature. Put the pork chops in a large Ziplock bag; put the cooled brine, seal, and coat the chops.

3. Put it in a 13x9-in. Baking dish then cools it in the fridge within 8-12 hours. Pat-dry the chops from the brine, then discard the brine. Drizzle both sides of chops using oil.

4. Mix the rub fixings in a small bowl, then rub it onto pork chops. Let stand at room temperature 30 minutes.

5. Grill chops on an oiled rack, covered, over medium heat 4-6 minutes on each side or until a thermometer read 145°. Let stand 5 minutes before serving.

Nutrition:

Calories: 300

Fat: 18g

Cholesterol: 72mg

Sodium: 130mg

Carbohydrate: 5g

Protein: 30g

62. Peppered Ribeye Steaks

Preparation Time: 10 minutes

Cooking Time: 10 minutes

Servings: 8

Ingredients:

- 1 tbsp garlic powder
- 1 tbsp paprika
- 2 tsp dried ground thyme

- 2 tsp dried ground oregano
- 1-1/2 tsp kosher salt
- 1-1/2 tsp pepper
- 1 tsp lemon-pepper seasoning
-
- 1 tsp cayenne pepper
- 1 tsp crushed red pepper flakes
- 4 beef ribeye steaks

Directions:

1. Mix all the seasonings, then sprinkle it over the steaks.
2. Marinate it in the fridge within 1 hour or up to 24 hours. Remove and pat dry with paper towels, but leave the garlic mixture on steaks as possible.
3. Grill the steaks, covered, turning occasionally.
4. Move the steaks to direct heat; continue to grill until meat reaches desired doneness.
5. Let it cool down within 5 minutes before slicing and serve.

Nutrition:

Calories: 257

Fat: 18g

Cholesterol: 67mg

Sodium: 453mg

Carbohydrate: 2g

Protein: 21g

63. Mushroom Braised Pot Roast

Preparation Time: 10 minutes

Cooking Time: 1 hour 30 minutes

Servings: 10

Ingredients:

- 4 pounds chuck roast
- 2 tablespoons vegetable oil
- 1/2 teaspoon salt
- 1/4 teaspoon pepper
- 1 cup chopped onion
- 2 cups beef broth
- 2 tablespoons gravy master
- 2 tablespoons butter
- 1-pound cremini mushrooms sliced or white button mushrooms
- 1/2 teaspoon salt

Directions:

1. Rub the roast with salt plus pepper, then put the vegetable oil in the Instant Pot and brown the roast all over.

2. Put 1 chopped onion with 2 cups of beef broth and 2 tablespoons of Gravy Master. Use the meat-setting button within 90 minutes.

3. Let the pot to release by using the natural release method.

4. While the pot is releasing the pressure, naturally sauté 1 pound of sliced mushrooms butter.

5. Put 1/2 teaspoon of salt to the mushrooms while sautéing.

6. When mushrooms are cooked through, add to the roast.

Nutrition:

Calories: 392

Carbohydrates: 3g

Protein: 37g

Fat: 26g

Cholesterol: 131mg

Sodium: 782mg

Potassium: 862mg

Sugar: 1g

64. Outback Steak House Grilled Pork chops

Preparation time: 15 minutes

Cooking time: 25 minutes

Servings: 2

Ingredients:

- 2 pieces of boneless loin pork chops
- 2 tsp. of steak rub
- 1/4 cup of Outback Steakhouse Marmalade Sauce

For Creole Marmalade Sauce:

- 1/4 cup of honey
- 1/4 cup of sweet orange marmalade
- 1/2 tsp. of dry mustard

For Steak Rub:

- 1/2 tsp. of coriander
- 2 tsp. of fresh ground black pepper
- 4-6 tsp. of sea salt (depending on taste)
- 1 tsp. of red cayenne pepper
- 1/2 tsp. of turmeric
- 4 tsp. of paprika
- 1 tsp. of onion powder
- 1 tsp. of garlic powder

Directions:

1. With the help of a paper towel, dry the pork chops.

2. Sprinkle the prepared rub over chops; rub them with some olive oil. Let them sit for 10 minutes.

3. Meanwhile, warm the grill on High for 10 minutes.

4. Switch grill down to medium-high, position grill chops on the rack for 3-4 minutes, or until grill marks appear.

5. Without flipping them over, turn the pork chop at 90 degrees. Cook for another three, four minutes, then flip over and cook for another six to eight minutes.

6. Remove from grill and let rest for around 5 minutes on a platter.

7. In the meantime, make the sauce and serve with the Creole marmalade.

Nutrition:

Calories 416

Proteins 20g

Carbs 4g

Fat 10g

Fiber 5g

65. Holiday Inn Victorville Pork Egg Roll in a Bowl

Preparation time: 15 minutes

Cooking time: 30 minutes

Servings: 4

Ingredients:

- 2 tbsp. of sesame oil
- 3 cloves minced of garlic
- 1/2 cup of onion, diced
- 5 pieces of green onions (white and green parts), sliced on a bias
- 4 cups of minced pork
- 1/2 tsp. of ground ginger
- Sea salt and black pepper, to taste
- 1 tbsp. of Sirach (or chili sauce)
- 1 cup of coleslaw mix
- Coconut Aminos: 3 tbsp. of coconut aminos or gluten-free soy sauce
- 1 tbsp. of rice vinegar, unseasoned
- 2 tbsp. of toasted sesame seeds

Directions:

Warm the sesame oil over a medium-high flame in a wide skillet.

1. Add the green onions into the garlic, white portion of onion. Sauté until onions become translucent and garlic becomes fragrant.

2. Add the minced pork, sea salt, ground ginger, black pepper, and Sriracha

3. Sauté until the pork is thoroughly cooked.

4. Add the mixture of coleslaw, coconut aminos, and vinegar. Sauté until coleslaw becomes soft.

5. Sprinkle with sesame seeds, green onions for finishing.

Nutrition:

Calories 254

Proteins 20g

Carbs 7g

Fat 20g

Fiber 1.5g

66. Fudpuckers Bacon-wrapped Tuna

Preparation time: 15 minutes

Cooking time: 40 minutes

Servings: 4

Ingredients:

- 4 finely sliced of bacon
- 2 cups of Tuna fillets

- 1/4 cup of Worcestershire sauce
- 1/2 cup of soy sauce
- Black pepper
- Sea salt to taste
- 4 tbsp. of honey

Directions:

1. To secure the bacon into Tuna, an easy way to wrap Tuna is to use a toothpick to secure Tuna's bacon.
2. Put the grill on. To make a basting sauce, mixing honey, soy sauce, and Worcestershire sauce. Rub this mix on Tuna.
3. Start cooking the bacon-wrapped Tuna until bacon starts getting crispy. Flip it.
4. Cook to your taste, until done. Medium to medium-rare is suggested.
5. Brush with a basting sauce, again.
6. Until slicing, sprinkle the Tuna gently with freshly ground black pepper.

Nutrition:

Calories 540

Proteins 30g

Carbs 18g

Fat 8g

Fiber 0g

67. Tojo's Bar and Grill Orange Roast Pork Loin Recipe

Preparation time: 15 minutes

Cooking time: 40 minutes

Servings: 4

Ingredients:

- 12 cups of pork loin
- 2 small oranges, juiced
- 3 tbsp. of fresh rosemary

- 5 cloves sliced of garlic
- 3 tbsp. of olive oil
- Freshly ground black pepper
- Salt
- 2 tbsp. of paprika

Directions:

1. Let the oven preheat to 400F.
2. Brush the pork with olive oil all over and spritz with sea salt, paprika pepper. Rub the garlic and rosemary on the bacon.
3. Mix the liquid ingredients. Put the pork loin in a big baking dish, and pour over the pork 1/2 of lime juices.
4. Bake for 1 hour in the oven. Place any of the residual juices over the pork loin every 20 minutes, then turn the pork loin.
5. Remove from the oven until pork loin hits 145F at its internal temperature
6. Rest it for a while. Meanwhile, it will keep cooking once it is out of the oven.

Nutrition:

Calories 302

Proteins 23g

Carbs 7g

Fat 16g

Fiber 2g

Chapter 7. Vegetables

68. Five Cheese Ziti Al Forno

Preparation time: 10 minutes

Cooking time: 50 minutes

Servings: 12

Ingredients:

- Ziti
- 1-pound dry ziti pasta
- 1½ quarts marinara sauce or Sunday gravy
- 1-quart alfredo sauce
- 1 cup ricotta cheese
- 2 cups mozzarella cheese, shredded
- 1 cup fontina cheese, shredded
- 1½ cups parmesan cheese
- 2 teaspoons Italian seasoning
- 1 teaspoon garlic powder

Topping:

- 2 cups mozzarella cheese, shredded
- ½ cup Italian breadcrumbs
- 3 tablespoons Romano cheese, shredded
- 3 tablespoons parmesan cheese

- 1 tablespoon fresh garlic, chopped
- 3 tablespoons Italian parsley, chopped
- 3 tablespoons olive oil

Directions:

1. Preheat oven to 375°F. Spray a 9×13 or 15×10 baking dish with nonstick cooking spray.
2. Cook ziti according to package directions. Drain and set aside.
3. Mix the marinara sauce, alfredo sauce, ricotta, mozzarella, fontina, parmesan, Italian seasoning, and garlic powder in a large mixing bowl.
4. Add the ziti to the sauce, then combine well. Pour into the baking dish—spread mozzarella on top.
5. To make the topping, combine the cheeses, breadcrumbs, fresh garlic, olive oil, and parsley in a bowl. Spread on top of the ziti.
6. Put it in the baking dish, then bake for 30–40 minutes or until the top is golden brown.

Nutrition:

Calories: 710

Carbs: 63g

Fat: 41g

Protein: 28g

69. Ravioli di Portobello

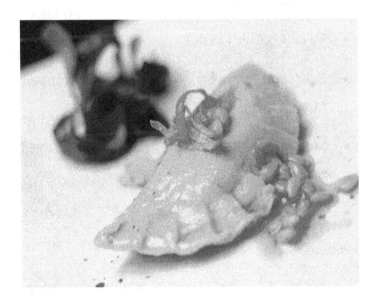

Preparation time: 60 minutes

Cooking time: 15 minutes

Servings: 8

Ingredients:

Ravioli dough:

- 3 cups flour
- 2 teaspoons salt
- 4 medium eggs
- ½ cup of cold water

Filling

- 32 ounces portobello mushrooms, finely diced
- 2 small onions, diced
- ½ cup butter (1 stick)
- Salt and pepper to taste
- Sun-dried tomato sauce
- 4 cups of milk
- ½ cup butter (1 stick)
- ½ cup flour
- 16 ounces smoked gouda cheese
- 6 sun-dried tomatoes, chopped
- Sliced green onion for serving
- 1-2 Italian tomato, diced, for serving

Directions:

1. Put the flour, mix in the salt on the working surface. With the fingers, make a hole in the middle of the flour. Add the eggs and mix in gently. Add water a small quantity at a time until a ball of dough forms.

2. Work the dough gently until smooth, and it doesn't stick to the fingers. Cover the dough with plastic wrap. Put in the fridge and let rest for 1 hour.

3. While the dough is resting, prepare the filling. In a large deep skillet, let the butter melt over medium heat.

4. Add the onions and sauté for 2 minutes or until fragrant and translucid. Add the mushrooms and continue stir-frying until soft, about 4-5 minutes.

5. Let the cooking juices evaporate for another 2-3 minutes. Remove and set aside.

6. Remove the dough to the fridge and let rest at room temperature for 10 minutes. Roll out the dough to ¼-inch thick pasta sheets using a pasta machine.

7. If you have ravioli forms, use them or use a glass or round cookie cutter of about 3-inch in diameter to cut the pasta.

8. To assemble a ravioli, take 2 pasta rounds, and lightly, with the fingers or a brush, moisten the edges with cold water.

9. Add about a tablespoon of the mushroom filling in the center of one of the two pasta rounds. Add the second round over and seal the edge with a fork, making sure it's seal all around. Make all the ravioli until all the pasta is used.

10. To cook the ravioli, bring some water to a boil in a large saucepan. Add some salt to the boiling water, about a tablespoon.

11. Add a few portions of ravioli at a time, and let cook until the ravioli come to the surface of the water, about 1-2 minutes.

12. Remove and transfer to a baking sheet layered with parchment paper on a single row to prevent the ravioli from sticking.

13. To make the sauce, let the butter melt in a large saucepan over medium-low heat. Add the flour and with a wooden spoon, stir to make a paste.

14. Add the milk gradually, whisking continuously until the sauce is smooth and has the desired consistency, about 4-5 minutes.

15. Add the cheese and sundried tomatoes. Stir until the cheese is completely melted. Put the ravioli in the saucepan, then stir to coat.

16. Serve immediately and garnish each place with sliced green onions and diced tomatoes, if desired.

Nutrition:

Calories: 670

Carbs: 74g

Fat: 30g

Protein: 25g

70. Eggplant Parmigiana

Preparation time: 2 hours

Cooking time: 30 minutes

Servings: 3

Ingredients:

- 1 large eggplant
- 1 egg
- ½ pound mozzarella cheese, shredded
- 1¾ cups milk
- 1 tablespoon clarified butter
- 2 teaspoons olive oil
- Flour (for dusting)
- 1 (24-ounce) jar marinara sauce
- 1 cup dry breadcrumbs
- ¾ cup parmesan cheese
- Salt and pepper, to taste

Directions:

1. Preheat oven to 350°F.
2. Prepare eggplant by blanching and peeling. Cut into ½-inch-thick slices. Put in a colander, then sprinkle with salt. Let drain for 30 minutes. Rinse and dry. Set aside.
3. Place egg, milk, and olive oil in a mixing bowl. In a separate bowl, mix breadcrumbs and parmesan, then in a third bowl, place flour.

4. Dip eggplant slices into the flour. Remove the excess, then dip into the egg wash. Let excess drip off, then toss into bread crumbs to coat thoroughly. Set aside to dry for about 1 hour.

5. Grease a baking pan with olive oil. Melt butter in a sauté pan and sauté the eggplant slices until golden on both sides. Transfer to the greased baking pan.

6. Cover the slices in mozzarella cheese and pour tomato sauce on top—Bake for 10 minutes. Let cool.

7. Sprinkle with oregano. Best served with pasta.

Nutrition:

Calories: 270

Carbs: 26g

Fat: 15g Protein: 8g

71. Gnocchi with Spicy Tomato and Wine Sauce

Preparation time: 10 minutes

Cooking time: 40 minutes

Servings: 4

Ingredients:

Sauce:

- 2 tablespoons extra virgin olive oil
- 6 fresh garlic cloves
- ½ teaspoon chili flakes
- 1 cup dry white wine
- 1 cup chicken broth
- 2 cans (14.5 ounces each) tomatoes
- ¼ cup fresh basil, chopped
- ¼ cup sweet, creamy butter, cut into 1-inch cubes, chilled
- ½ cup parmesan cheese, freshly grated

Pasta:

- 1-pound gnocchi
- Salt, to taste
- Black pepper, freshly crushed, to taste

Directions:

1. Put the olive oil, garlic, plus chili flakes in a cold pan and cook over medium heat.
2. Put the wine and broth and bring the mixture to a simmer.
3. After about 10 minutes, the broth should be halved. When that happens, add in the tomatoes and basil and then let the sauce continue simmering for another 30 minutes.

4. Set aside the sauce once it thickens to cool for 3 minutes.

5. After 3 minutes, place the sauce in a blender, and add the butter and parmesan. Purée everything together and set aside.

6. Prepare the pasta by boiling the gnocchi in a large pot. When it is cooked, strain the pasta and mix with the sauce.

7. Transfer everything to a plate and serve.

Nutrition:

Calories: 266

Carbs: 33g

Fat: 0g

Protein: 10g

Chapter 8. Soups & Stews

72. Outback's French Onion Soup

Preparation Time: 15 minutes

Cooking Time: 50 minutes

Servings: 4

Ingredients:

- 2 cups sweet yellow onion, quartered and sliced
- ½ cup sweet cream butter
- ½ teaspoon salt
- 1 tablespoon flour
- 4 cups beef stock
- 1 tablespoon fresh thyme
- 1 teaspoon coarse ground black pepper
- 4 baguette slices, approximately ½-inch thick
- 8 slices Provolone cheese

Directions:

1. Melt the butter in a stockpot under medium heat.
2. Over medium heat, melt the butter in a stockpot.
3. Put the onions plus salt, and cook for 3 minutes. Put the flour and stir.

4. Add the beef stock, increase the heat to medium-high, and bring to a boil. Let boil for 1 minute.

5. Reduce heat to the low, season with black pepper and thyme. Cover for 25-30 minutes, and simmer.

6. Toast the baguette slices until medium golden brown while the soup is simmering. Make sure every piece fit comfortably in your bowl of soup.

7. Warm the broiler.

8. Ladle in ovenproof serving bowls when the soup is done simmering.

9. Place a slice of baguette at the top of each bowl and two pieces of Provolone cheese. Put in the broiler for 1-2 minutes, or until the cheese is well melted and caramelized lightly. Serve.

Nutrition:

Calories: 420

Fat: 29 g

Protein: 19 g

Carbs: 21 g

73. Red Lobster's Clam Chowder

Preparation Time: 20 minutes

Cooking Time: 30 minutes

Servings: 8

Ingredients:

- 2 tablespoons butter
- 1 cup onion, diced
- ½ cup leek, white part, thinly sliced
- ¼ teaspoon garlic, minced
- ½ cup celery, diced
- 2 tablespoons flour
- 4 cups of milk
- 1 cup clams with juice, diced
- 1 cup potato, diced
- 1 tablespoon salt
- ¼ teaspoon white pepper
- 1 teaspoon dried thyme
- ½ cup heavy cream
- Saltine crackers for serving

Directions:

1. In a pot, sauté the onion, leek, garlic, and celery in butter over medium heat.
2. Remove the vegetables from the heat after 3 minutes and add the flour.
3. Whisk in the milk and clam juice.

4. Put back the mixture to the heat and bring it to a boil.

5. Put the potatoes, thyme, salt, and pepper, adjust the heat to low, and let the mixture simmer. Continue mixing for another 10 minutes while the soup is simmering.

6. Add in the clams and let the mixture simmer for 5 to 8 minutes, or until the clams are cooked.

7. Add the heavy cream and cook for a few more minutes.

8. Transfer the soup to a bowl and serve with saltine crackers.

Nutrition:

Calories: 436.1

Fat: 26.5 g

Protein: 20.3 g

Carbs: 30.1 g

74. Carrabba's Mama Mandola Sicilian Chicken Soup

Preparation Time: 15 minutes

Cooking Time: 8 hours

Servings: 10

Ingredients:

- 4 carrots, peeled, diced
- 4 stalks celery, diced
- 1 green bell pepper, cored, diced
- 2 medium white potatoes, diced
- 1 white onion, diced
- 3 cloves garlic, minced
- 1 can (14.5 ounces) tomatoes, diced, with juice
- 1 tablespoon fresh parsley
- 1 teaspoon Italian seasoning
- ½ teaspoon white pepper
- crushed red pepper flakes
- 2 boneless skinless chicken breasts, shredded
- 32-ounces containers chicken stock
- 1 ½ teaspoons salt
- 1-pound Ditalini pasta

Directions:

1. Dice and chop the vegetables as instructed.
2. Place them in a slow cooker and sprinkle with the parsley, seasoning, and white and red pepper. Mix everything.
3. Add the shredded chicken and stock and remix it.
4. Cover the mixture and cook it for 8 hours on low heat.

5. When the soup is nearly cooked, bring a salt-and-water mixture to a boil to cook the pasta.

6. Add the cooked pasta to the soup. Cook for another 5 minutes and serve.

Nutrition:

Calories: 320

Fat: 0 g

Protein: 13 g

Carbs: 57 g

75. Carrabba's Sausage and Lentil Soup

Preparation Time: 10 minutes

Cooking Time: 1 hour 5 minutes

Servings: 6

Ingredients:

- 1-pound Italian sausages
- 1 large onion, diced
- 1 stalk celery, diced
- 2 large carrots, diced
- 1 small zucchini, diced
- 6 cups low sodium chicken broth
- 2 cans (14.5 ounces each) tomatoes, chopped, with juice

- 2 cups dry lentils
- 2–3 garlic cloves, minced
- 1 ½ teaspoons salt
- 1 teaspoon black pepper
- 1-3 pinches red pepper flakes
- 1 teaspoon dry basil
- ½ teaspoon dry oregano
- ½ teaspoon parsley
- ½ teaspoon dry thyme
- Parmesan cheese for garnishing

Directions:

1. Preheat the oven to 350°F. Place sausages on a baking dish and poke a few holes in each link with a fork. Bake until the sausages are finished (around 20-30 minutes)

2. Let the sausages cool down and slice.

3. Chop and thin the ingredients as set out in the list of ingredients.

4. Put all the fixings in a large pot, except for the Parmesan cheese.

5. Let the mixture simmer for an hour, adding water where necessary to reduce thickness. Puree a portion of the soup, and return it if you want a thicker soup.

6. Before serving, ladle the soup in bowls and garnish with parmesan cheese.

Nutrition:

Calories: 221

Fat: 10 g

Protein: 13 g

Carbs: 20 g

76. Denny's Vegetable and Beef Barley Soup

Preparation Time: 10 minutes

Cooking Time: 40 minutes

Servings: 4

Ingredients:

- ½ pound ground beef
- 16 ounces frozen mixed vegetables
- 1 can (14.5 ounces) tomatoes, diced, with juice
- ¼ cup barley
- 2-ounce beef broth
- Salt and pepper

Directions:

1. Place the ground beef in a pot and cook until brown.

2. Add in the vegetables, tomatoes, barley, and broth, and bring the entire mixture to a simmer.

3. Put the salt plus pepper for seasoning and leave the mixture to simmer for at least 40 minutes.

4. Ladle the soup into bowls and serve. The longer you leave the soup to simmer, the better it will taste.

Nutrition:

Calories: 244.5

Fat: 11.4 g

Protein: 20 g

Carbs: 17.1 g

Chapter 9. Snacks

77. Taco Bell Bean Burrito

Preparation Time: 15 minutes

Cooking Time: 25-35 minutes

Servings: 5–6

Ingredients:

Taco Bell Red Sauce:

- 2 8-ounce can of tomato sauce
- 1 cup of water
- 2 tsp. of dried minced onions
- 2 tbsp. of white vinegar

- 1/2 tsp. of paprika
- 1/2 tsp. of chili powder
- 1/2 tsp. of cayenne pepper
- 1 tsp. of garlic
- Salt
- 1/2 tsp. of sugar
- 2 tsp. of ground cumin
- 1 tsp. of garlic powder

For Assembly:

- 6 (8") tortillas
- 2 (16 ounces) can of refry beans
- 1 cup of shredded cheddar cheese
- 1/2 cup of diced onion

Directions:

Taco Bell Red Sauce:

1. Over medium heat, combine and simmer the first seven ingredients for around 25 minutes.
2. Meanwhile, reheat fried beans on low heat in a small pan.

Assembly:

1. Lay tortilla on a warm pan and heat on both sides, put the refried beans, sauce, onions, cheese, and fold the tortilla. Serve and enjoy.

Nutrition:

Calories: 370

Fat: 11g

Carbs: 56g

Protein: 15g

78. Taco Bell Beefy 5-Layer Burrito

Preparation Time: 15 minutes

Cooking Time: 25-30 minutes

Servings: 6

Ingredients:

Homemade taco seasoning:

- 2 tablespoon of corn starch
- 2 tablespoons of all-purpose flour
- 3 1/2 teaspoons of granulated beef bouillon
- 1 teaspoon of garlic powder
- 1 1/2 teaspoon of paprika
- 1 teaspoon of granulated sugar
- 1 teaspoon of chili powder
- 1 teaspoon of cumin
- 1 teaspoon of onion powder

- ¼ teaspoon of natural unsweetened cocoa powder

For ground beef:

- ½ lb. of ground beef

Homemade taco seasoning:

- 2/3 cup of water

Assembly:

- 6 pieces of flour tortillas
- 1 cup of salsa con queso
- 1 1/2 cups of refried beans
- 1 cup of shredded Mexican cheese
- 1 cup of sour cream

Directions:

Taco Seasoning:

2. Mix all the homemade taco seasoning ingredients in a bowl and mix until well combined.
3. Ground beef Tacos:

4. Heat oil in a pan and sauté and brown ground beef. Remove excess fat. Add water to the pan and the taco seasoning you just made.

5. Boil, then lower down to a simmering heat. Let it cook within 15 minutes, stirring constantly. While waiting, reheat fried beans over low heat in a small pan.

Assembly:

1. Lay tortilla on a warm pan and heat on both sides, spread a salsa con queso, put beef, refried beans, sauce, onions, shredded Mexican cheese, and fold the tortilla. Serve and enjoy.

Nutrition:

Calories: 490

Fat: 18g

Carbs: 63g

Protein: 18g

79. Taco Bell Chicken Burrito

Preparation Time: 25–30 minutes

Cooking Time: 35 minutes

Servings: 3

Ingredients:

- 1 lb. of boneless skinless chicken breasts
- 2 (8 ounces) cans of tomato sauce
- 1 tablespoon of olive oil
- 2 teaspoons of white vinegar
- 3 garlic cloves (minced)
- ½ teaspoon of sugar
- 1 teaspoon of ground cumin
- 2 teaspoons of oregano
- Salt and pepper (to taste)
- 4 teaspoons of chili powder
- Lime and Cilantro Rice
- ½ tablespoon of butter
- 2 cups of chicken broth
- ¼ teaspoon of cumin
- 1 cup of long-grain white rice
- ¾ teaspoon of salt
- ¼ teaspoon of ground black pepper
- 2 tablespoons of chopped cilantro
- Juice and zest of 1 lime

Avocado-Ranch Dressing:

- ½ avocado

- ¼ cup of ranch dressing
- 1/8 cup of buttermilk
- 2 tablespoons of sour cream
- 1 teaspoon of salt

For assembly:

- 6 pieces of flour tortillas
- 2 cups of shredded cheddar cheese

Directions:

2. Combine ranch dressing, avocado, buttermilk, sour cream, and salt in a blender and pulse until it becomes smooth. Chill while not in use.

3. In a large pan, heat oil and put in chicken breasts, add tomato sauce and simmer until the chicken is cooked thoroughly.

4. Transfer it to a flat dish and shred. Put it back to the sauce and continue simmering until the most liquid's absorbed.

5. Then, start making the lime-cilantro rice by melting butter in a saucepan. Put in your rice grains and coat with butter.

6. Add chicken broth, lime juice, zest, pepper, salt, and cumin. Boil and lower down to a simmering heat. Cook until the rice is tender.

7. Wrap the tortilla in a damp towel and heat in the microwave for 3–5 minutes.
8. Lay the tortilla on a plate, add dressing, chicken rice, and lastly, top with shredded cheese. Fold, serve, and enjoy.

Nutrition:

Calories: 350

Fat: 10g

Carbs: 47g

Protein: 19g

80. Taco Bell Cheese Potato Burrito

Preparation Time: 15-25 minutes

Cooking Time: 25 -30 minutes

Servings: 4

Ingredients:

Homemade taco seasoning:

- 2 tablespoon of corn starch
- 2 tablespoons of all-purpose flour
- 3 1/2 teaspoons of granulated beef bouillon
- 1 teaspoon of garlic powder

- 1 1/2 teaspoon of paprika
- 1 teaspoon of granulated sugar
- 1 teaspoon of chili powder
- 1 teaspoon of cumin
- 1 teaspoon of onion powder
- ¼ teaspoon of natural unsweetened cocoa powder

For ground beef:

- ½ lb. of ground beef
- 2/3 cup of water

Potato filling:

- Oil for frying
- 3/4-pound of potatoes (about 2 medium), peeled and cut into 1/2-in. cubes

Assembly:

- 8 flour tortillas (10 inches), warmed
- 4 cups of shredded Mexican cheese blend

Directions:

1. Taco Seasoning: Add all the ingredients under the homemade taco seasoning in a bowl and mix until well combined.

2. Ground beef Tacos: Heat oil in a pan and sauté and brown ground beef. Remove excess fat.

3. Add water to the pan and the taco seasoning you just made. Bring to a boil, then lower down to a simmering heat.

4. Cook within 15 minutes, stirring constantly. At the same time, reheat fried beans to low heat in a pan.

5. For the Potato filling, heat oil to 200°C, then fry potatoes per batch until crispy outside and tender inside.

6. Assembly: Lay tortilla on a warm pan and heat both sides; add ground meat, shredded Mexican cheese, and potatoes. And fold the tortilla. Serve and enjoy.

Nutrition:

Calories: 480

Fat: 22g

Carbs: 55g

Protein: 18g

81. Taco Bell Black Bean Burrito

Preparation Time: 5 minutes

Cooking Time: 5 minutes

Servings: 6

Ingredients:

- 1 tablespoon of olive oil
- 1 can of black beans
- 1 small onion, chopped
- 1 can of green salsa
- 1/2 teaspoon of garlic powder
- 1/2 teaspoon of chili powder
- 1/2 teaspoon of ground cumin
- 6 pieces of a flour tortilla
- 2 ounces of shredded Mexican cheese blend (optional)
- 1 tomato, diced (optional)
- 1 avocado, sliced (optional)
- 1 cup of shredded lettuce (optional)

Directions:

1. Preheat oil in a saucepan over medium-low heat; cook onion in hot oil until tender, about 5 minutes.
2. Stir the black beans, green salsa, garlic powder, chili powder, and cumin with the onion. Adjust to low and cook the mixture at a simmer until it thickens, 5 to 10 minutes.

3. Lay the tortilla and put the beans mixture, Mexican cheese blend, tomato, avocado, and shredded lettuce.

Nutrition:

Calories: 380

Fat: 11g

Carbs: 56g

Protein: 14g

82. Taco Bell Chili Cheese Burrito

Preparation Time: 5 minutes

Cooking Time: 5 minutes

Servings: 6

Ingredients:

- 2 lbs. of ground beef
- 3 cups of water
- 2 cans refried beans
- 4 teaspoons of cornstarch
- ¼ cup of tomato paste
- 3 tablespoons of minced dried onions
- 2 teaspoons of cayenne pepper
- 3 teaspoons of distilled white vinegar
- 2 tablespoon of chili powder

- 2 teaspoons of salt
- 1/4 tablespoons of canned jalapeno slices
- 3 cups of shredded cheddar cheese
- 6 fresh burrito tortillas
- 1 cup of sour cream

Directions:

1. In a pan, heat oil and sauté the beef until brown. Drain off excess fat
2. In another pan, put the water and tomato paste. Stir.
3. Add in chili powder, cayenne pepper, salt, vinegar, onion, and cornstarch—Cook over medium heat. Lower down the heat after 5 minutes and add the jalapeno slices.
4. Put this tomato mixture to the browned beef. Reheat refried beans in the pan.
5. Gather all other ingredients for assembly. Lay a tortilla on a plate; add beef with tomato mix, cheese, refried beans, and sour cream.
6. Fold and heat in the microwave. Serve while hot.

Nutrition:

Calories: 370

Fat: 17g

Fiber: 4g

Carbs: 40g

Protein: 17g

83. Taco Bell Crunchy Taco

Preparation Time: 15 minutes

Cooking Time: 15 minutes

Servings: 4

Ingredients:

- 1 pound of lean ground beef (90% lean)
- 1 medium onion, finely chopped
- 1 garlic clove, minced
- 1/2 cup of water
- 1 tablespoon of chili powder
- 1-1/2 teaspoons of ground cumin
- 1/2 teaspoon of salt
- 1/2 teaspoon of paprika
- 1/2 teaspoon of pepper
- 1/4 teaspoon of dried oregano

- 1/4 tsp red pepper flakes, crushed
- 8 taco shells, warmed
- Toppings: shredded lettuce, chopped tomatoes, sliced green onions, and shredded cheddar cheese

Directions:

1. Cook the beef, onion, plus garlic on medium heat in a large frying pan, until the meat is no longer pink; drain. Stir in the water and seasonings.
2. Bring to a boil. Simmer, uncovered, within 5–10 minutes or until thickened.
3. Spoon the beef mixture into taco shells. Serve with toppings of your choice.

Nutrition:

Calories: 170

Fat: 9g

Carbs: 14g

Protein: 8g

84.   Taco Bell Nacho Supreme

Preparation Time: 15 minutes

Cooking Time: 15 minutes

Servings: 4

Ingredients:

- 1 packet taco seasoning
- 1lb. of ground beef
- 1 can of nacho cheese sauce
- 1 can of refried beans
- ¼ chopped onion
- 1 cup of diced tomato
- ½ cup of sour cream
- ¼ cup of jalapeno
- 5 cups of tortilla chips

Directions:

1. Preheat oven to 180°C.
2. In a pan, sauté and brown the beef. Drain the excess fat off from the beef and add taco seasoning, water, and tomatoes. Simmer until the liquid is absorbed.
3. Put the tortilla chips in a pan, add the meat mixture, refried beans, sour cream, and cheese mixture on top.

4. Bake for 15 minutes. Top with chopped onions and tomato. Pour another layer of cheese sauce if you desire.

Nutrition:

Calories: 411

Fat: 24g

Carbs: 41g

Protein: 10g

85. Taco Bell Burrito Supreme

Preparation Time: 30–35 minutes

Cooking Time: 25 minutes

Servings: 4–6

Ingredients:

- 1 1/2-pound of ground beef
- 1/2 cup of fresh or canned corn
- 1 can of diced tomatoes, undrained
- 1 cup of uncooked instant rice
- 1 teaspoon of salt
- 1/2 cup of water
- 1 envelope of taco seasoning

Toppings:

- 1 ½ cup of shredded Colby-Monterey Jack cheese
- 6 soft tortilla wraps
- ½ cup of Sour cream
- 12 pieces of sliced fresh jalapenos,
- 3 cups of shredded lettuce
- 3 pieces of tomatoes, diced
- 1 cup of onion

Directions:

1. Over medium heat, sauté the ground beef until brown and cooked thoroughly. Drain, then stir in the corn, tomatoes, water, rice, salt, and taco seasoning.
2. Boil, then lower down the heat to a simmer. Cook until rice is soft, around 15 minutes. Once cooked, remove from heat.
3. Assembly: Lay tortilla on a warm pan and heat on both sides, put rice-beef mixture, lettuce, tomato, onion, jalapenos, sour cream, cheese, and fold the tortilla. Serve and enjoy.

Nutrition:

Calories: 400

Fat: 15g

Carbs: 50g

Protein: 17g

Chapter 10. Desserts

86. Disney's Famous Churros

Preparation time: 20 minutes

Cooking time: 20 minutes

Servings: 20

Ingredients:

- 8 tablespoons butter
- 1 ¼ cups all-purpose flour
- ¾ teaspoon ground cinnamon, divided
- 3 organic eggs, large-sized
- 1 cup of water
- ½ cup of sugar
- 1 ½ cups vegetable or canola oil
- ¼ teaspoon salt

Directions:

1. Over medium heat in 1 ½ quart saucepan; combine the butter with ¼ teaspoon of cinnamon, water and salt; bring the mixture to a rolling boil.

2. Once done, decrease the heat to low. Slowly add the flour & vigorously stir until the mixture forms a ball. Immediately remove it from the heat and let rest for a couple of minutes.

3. Slowly add the eggs; stirring well after each addition until combined well; set aside until ready to use.

4. Then, over medium-high heat in a 1-quart saucepan or medium skillet; heat the oil to 350F.

5. Scoop the dough into a piping bag attached with a large star tip. Pipe 1" strip of dough over the saucepan, cut with a sharp knife and carefully drop into the hot oil. Repeat this step until churro bites fill the saucepan; ensure that there is some room available.

6. Fry the churro bites for a couple of minutes, until turn golden brown. Once done, remove them using a mesh spider strainer or slotted spoon.

7. Place the fried churro bites on a paper towel to drain.

8. Then, combine the sugar with ½ teaspoon of cinnamon in a medium-sized mixing bowl. Toss in the churro bites until nicely coated.

9. Place on a large-sized serving plate and serve with the dipping sauce, any of your favorite.

Nutrition:

Calories: 80

Carbs: 7g

Fat: 6g

Protein: 1g

87. Trolly Treats Churro Toffee

Preparation time: 10 minutes

Cooking time: 20 minutes

Servings: 12

Ingredients:

- 2 cups white sugar
- 4 sticks butter (approximately 2 cups)
- 3 bags Ghirardelli White Melting Wafers
- 1 teaspoon salt

For Topping:

- ½ cup granulated sugar combined with 1 tablespoon of ground cinnamon

Directions:

1. Line a large-sized baking sheet with parchment paper

2. Then, over medium heat in a large saucepan; combine the butter with sugar & salt, giving the ingredients a good stir until the butter is completely melted.

3. Continue to cook until you get a dark golden color. Cook & boil until the temperature reflects 285 F, stirring now and then.

4. As soon as the toffee reaches the temperature, immediately pour into the prepared baking sheet. Set aside and let set up in a refrigerator for 20 minutes.

5. Melt the wafers per the directions mentioned on the package & pour it on top of the toffee. Sprinkle with the sugar-cinnamon mixture; let set up for another 35 to 40 minutes. When set, break the toffee into pieces & enjoy.

Nutrition:

Calories: 190

Carbs: 20g

Fat: 12g

Protein: 1g

88. Rice Cereal Treats

Preparation time: 20 minutes

Cooking time: 40 minutes

Servings: 4

Ingredients:

- 6 cups Rice Krispies cereal
- 4 cups Jet-Puffed Miniature Marshmallows
- 3 tablespoons butter
- Chocolate Candy Melts
- Sprinkles

Directions:

1. Warm the butter until melted over low heat in a large saucepan. Add the marshmallows; give it a good stir until melted completely. Immediately remove it from the heat.
2. Add the Rice Krispies cereal; give it a good stir until coated well.
3. Evenly press the mixture into a 13x9x2" pan lightly coated with the cooking spray, using wax paper or buttered spatula. Let cool.
4. Cut into desired shapes using a Mickey Mouse cookie cutter.
5. Then, heat the chocolate in a microwave until melted. Start with a 30 second time & then add time in 15-second increments.

6. Dip the top of your Rice Krispy Treat into the chocolate. Put it on a pan with parchment paper or wax paper & add the sprinkles. Serve and enjoy.

Nutrition:

Calories: 120

Carbs: 26g

Fat: 1g

Protein: 1g

89. German Pavilion Caramel Corn

Preparation time: 20 minutes

Cooking time: 25 minutes

Servings: 6

Ingredients:

- ½ cup popcorn kernels
- 2 cups of sugar
- 1 cup light corn syrup
- 1 ½ stick salted butter
- 1 can evaporate milk
- ¼ cup of coconut oil
- 1 teaspoon kosher salt

Directions:

1. Warm the coconut oil until melted over medium to high heat in a deep pot with a lid.

2. Once done, add 2 to 3 kernels of the popcorn into the hot pot. Once they begin to pop, scoop them out & dump in the leftover kernels.

3. Quickly shake the pot to disperse the kernels evenly. Cover the pot with a lid & immediately remove it from the heat.

4. Wait for half a minute, and then put the pot over the heat again. Once the kernels begin to pop vigorously, start shaking the pot until the popping stops or slows down.

5. Put the popcorn into a large bowl immediately.

6. Wipe the popcorn pot out and then add 1 stick of butter followed by evaporated milk, sugar, corn syrup, and kosher salt, giving the ingredients a good stir.

7. Boil the mixture over high heat.

8. Continue to stir the ingredients until the candy thermometer reflects 266 F, mixing the ingredients' entire time.

9. Remove, then stir in the additional stick of butter.

10. The moment it melts, immediately dump the popcorn into the pot & stir until nicely coated.

11. Put the popcorn onto a sheet pan and evenly spread it, then let completely cool, then break it into smaller bits. Serve and enjoy.

Nutrition:

Calories: 120

Carbs: 21g

Fat: 4g

Protein: 0g

90. Ginger Bread Popcorn

Preparation time: 20 minutes

Cooking time: 20 minutes

Servings: 4

Ingredients:

- ½ cup butter
- 1 bag Homestyle popcorn
- ¼ cup each of molasses & corn syrup
- 1 teaspoon vanilla
- ¾ cup packed brown sugar
- Wilton drizzle pouches; green and red
- ½ teaspoon each of:
- ground ginger

- cinnamon
- ground cloves
- baking soda
- ¼ teaspoon salt

Directions:

1. Preheat your oven to 250 F.
2. Pop the popcorn and pour them into a large-sized mixing bowl.
3. Prepare a large-sized cookie sheet with a silicone baking mat.
4. Then, over moderate heat in a large saucepan, heat the butter until melted, and add the molasses, ginger, corn syrup, brown sugar, ground cloves, cinnamon, and salt.
5. Boil the mixture within 3 to 5 minutes, stirring the ingredients now and then.
6. Remove the mixture from heat. Add the baking soda and vanilla.
7. Put the sauce on top of the popcorn immediately; toss to coat.
8. Spread the popcorn on the prepared cookie sheet & place them in the oven for an hour.
9. To prevent the popcorn from burning, don't forget to toss them every 15 minutes.

10. Let cool for an hour, and then drizzle the Wilton coating on top of the popcorn.

11. Gently break the popcorn & store them in an airtight container.

Nutrition:

Calories: 130

Carbs: 18g

Fat: 7g

Protein: 1g

91. Port Orleans Beignets

Preparation time: 35 minutes

Cooking time: 10 minutes

Servings: 20

Ingredients:

- 1-pound gluten-free pizza crust mix
- ½ cup plus 2 tablespoons apple juice
- 1 ½ teaspoon dry active yeast
- ¼ cup applesauce, unsweetened

- 2 ½ teaspoons powdered egg replacer, gluten-free
- ½ teaspoon canola oil
- A pinch of ground cinnamon
- ½ cup plus 2 tablespoons warm water
- 3 tablespoons sugar
- ¼ teaspoon salt
- Confectioners' sugar for finishing

Directions:

1. Combine the yeast with warm water in a small-sized mixing bowl, set aside for a couple of minutes.

2. Combine the apple juice with egg replacer, applesauce, oil, sugar, cinnamon & salt in the bowl of an electric mixer attached with a paddle attachment. Continue to mix until combined well.

3. Slowly add the pizza crust mix until soft dough forms. Put the dough onto a working surface lightly dusted with the leftover pizza crust mix.

4. Knead until the dough is no longer sticky but ensure that it's still soft.

5. Roll the dough out to approximately ¼" thickness & then cut into 2×3" pieces. Set aside for 20 minutes at room temperature.

6. Fill a deep-sided pot with approximately 2" of oil and heat it over medium heat.

7. Lightly press the beignets until slightly flatten. Add some of the beignets to the hot oil & fry until both sides turn golden brown, turning once or twice.

8. Using a slotted spoon, remove from the hot oil & place them on a paper towel-lined baking sheet. Just before serving, don't forget to dust with a generous amount of the confectioners' sugar.

Nutrition:

Calories: 71

Carbs: 9g

Fat: 4g

Protein: 1g

92. Pineapple Upside Down Cakes

Preparation time: 20 minutes

Cooking time: 20 minutes

Servings: 10

Ingredients:

20 oz. can pineapple, crushed

- 1 box yellow cake mix
- 10 tablespoons brown sugar
- 5 maraschino cherries
- Oil and eggs per the instructions mentioned on the box

Directions:

1. Grease 10 ramekins. Drain the crushed pineapple, set the juice aside.
2. Prepare the cake mix per the directions mentioned on the box, substituting the pineapple juice for water.
3. Spoon approximately 1 tablespoon of the brown sugar into each ramekin. Evenly spread using a large spoon.
4. Spoon approximately 1 tablespoon of crushed pineapple into each ramekin & evenly spread using a spoon.
5. Cut the maraschino cherries into half & place one half into each ramekin.
6. Add the leftover crushed pineapple to the cake batter; continue to mix until incorporated well.
7. Spoon the cake batter into the 10 ramekins; ensure that they all are filled equally.
8. Bake within 15 to 17 minutes, at 350 F.

9. Let completely cool. Once done, run a knife around the outside edge & carefully release the cake from the ramekins.

10. Put them on a large plate and top with the Pineapple Sherbet. Serve immediately & enjoy.

Nutrition:

Calories: 440

Carbs: 65g

Fat: 18g

Protein: 5g

93. Liberty Tree Tavern Ooey Gooey Toffee Cake

Preparation time: 10 minutes

Cooking time: 40 minutes

Servings: 4

Ingredients:

For Cake Bottom:

- 1 box of yellow cake mix
- ½ cup butter (approximately 1 stick)

- 1 organic egg, large

For Cake Filling:

- 1 cup Heath Bar pieces
- 8 ounces cream cheese
- 1 teaspoon vanilla extract
- 3 organic eggs, large
- 1 cup semi-sweet chocolate chips
- ¼ cup butter
- 1-pound sugar, powdered

Directions:

For Cake Bottom:

1. Grease a 13X9" baking pan; set aside until ready to use.
2. Then, combine the real ingredients in a large-sized mixing bowl until mixed well. Once done, put the prepared mixture into the baking pan.

For Filling:

1. Put the cream cheese in a mixer. Slowly add vanilla and eggs.
2. Add butter & mix until combined well.
3. Slowly add the powdered sugar and then add the Heath Bar pieces and chocolate chips; mix well.

4. Pour the prepared mixture over the Ooey Gooey Toffee Cake Bottom. Bake for 30 to 35 minutes, at 325 F.

Nutrition:

Calories: 220

Carbs: 33g

Fat: 9g

Protein: 2g

94. Triple Chocolate Meltdown

Preparation Time: 1 hour

Cooking time: 30 minutes

Servings: 8

Ingredients:

- 2 cups heavy cream, divided
- 1 cup white chocolate chips
- 1 cup semi-sweet chocolate chips
- 1-pound bittersweet chocolate, chopped
- ½ cup butter softened
- 6 eggs
- 1 ½ cups of sugar
- 1 ½ cups all-purpose flour
- Ice cream, for serving

Directions:

1. Preheat the oven to 400°F.

2. Prepare 8 ramekins by first coating the inside with butter, then sprinkle them with flour, so the bottom and sides are covered. Place them on a baking tray.

3. In a saucepan, bring 1 cup of heavy cream to a simmer. Remove it from the heat and add the white chocolate chips, stirring until the chocolate is melted and the mixture is smooth.

4. Allow it to cool down within half an hour, stirring occasionally. Repeat with the other cup of cream and the semi-sweet chocolate chips.

5. In a double boiler, combine the bittersweet chocolate with the softened butter until melted and smooth. Remove and allow to cool down for about 10 minutes.

6. Beat the eggs and the sugar in a mixing bowl for about 2 minutes, or until the mixture is foamy. Fold in the bittersweet chocolate mixture.

7. Beat to low the flour half a cup simultaneously in the mixer, being careful not to overmix the batter.

8. Put the batter evenly into the prepared ramekins and place the baking tray in the oven—Bake for about 18 minutes.

9. Remove, and let the ramekins sit on the tray for 2–3 minutes and then invert them onto serving plates.

10. Drizzle some semi-sweet and white chocolate sauces over the top and serve with a scoop of ice cream.

Nutrition:

Calories: 421

Fat: 13 g

Carbs: 22 g

Protein: 24.0 g

Sodium: 311 mg

95.   Chocolate Mousse Dessert Shooter

Preparation Time: 30 minutes

Cooking time: 2 minutes

Servings: 4

Ingredients:

- 2 tablespoons butter
- 6 ounces' semi-sweet chocolate chips (1 cup), divided
- 2 eggs
- 1 teaspoon vanilla
- 8 Oreo cookies
- ½ cup prepared fudge sauce
- 2 tablespoons sugar
- ½ cup heavy cream
- Canned whipped cream

Directions:

1. Melt the butter and all but 1 tablespoon of the chocolate chips in a double boiler.
2. When they are melted, stir in the vanilla and remove from the heat.
3. Whisk in the egg yolks, then the egg whites until they form soft peaks, and then fold them into the chocolate mixture.

4. Beat the sugar and heavy cream in a separate bowl until it forms stiff peaks or the consistency you desire. Fold this into the chocolate mixture.

5. Crush the remaining chocolate chips into small pieces and stir them into the chocolate.

6. Crush the Oreos. Spoon the cookie crumbs into the bottom of your cup and pat them down. Layer the chocolate mixture on top.

7. Finish with whipped cream and either more chocolate chips or Oreo mixture. Store in the refrigerator until ready to serve.

Nutrition:

Calories: 389

Fat: 11.6 g

Carbs: 25. 2 g

Protein: 39.0 g

Sodium: 222 mg

96. Cinnamon Apple Turnover

Preparation Time: 10 minutes

Cooking time: 25 minutes

Servings: 6

Ingredients:

- 1 large Granny Smith apple, diced
- ½ teaspoon cornstarch
- ¼ teaspoon cinnamon
- Dash ground nutmeg
- ¼ cup brown sugar
- ¼ cup applesauce
- ¼ teaspoon vanilla extract
- 1 tablespoon butter, melted
- 1 sheet of puff pastry, thawed
- Whipped cream, to serve

Directions:

1. Preheat the oven to 400°F.
2. Assemble a baking sheet by spraying it with non-stick cooking spray or using a bit of oil on a paper towel.
3. In a mixing bowl, mix the apples, cornstarch, cinnamon, nutmeg, and brown sugar. Stir to make sure the apples are well covered with the spices. Then stir in the applesauce and the vanilla.

4. Layout your puff pastry and cut it into squares. You should be able to make 4 or 6 depending on how big you want your turnovers to be and how big your pastry is.

5. Place some of the apple mixtures in each square's center and fold the corners of the pastry up to make a pocket. Pinch the edges together to seal. Then brush a bit of the melted butter over the top to give the turnovers that nice brown color.

6. Put the filled pastry onto the prepared baking pan and transfer it to the preheated oven. Bake 20–25 minutes, or until they become a golden brown.

7. You can serve it with vanilla ice cream whipped cream.

Nutrition:

Calories: 235

Fat: 15.8 g

Carbs: 20. 5 g

Protein: 26 g

Sodium: 109 mg

97. Cherry Chocolate Cobbler

Preparation Time: 10 minutes

Cooking time: 45 minutes

Servings: 8

Ingredients:

- 1½ cups all-purpose flour
- ½ cup of sugar
- 2 teaspoons baking powder
- ½ teaspoon salt
- ¼ cup butter
- 6 ounces' semi-sweet chocolate morsels
- ¼ cup milk
- 1 egg, beaten
- 21 ounces' cherry pie filling
- ½ cup finely chopped nuts

Directions:

1. Preheat the oven to 350°F.
2. Mix the baking powder, flour, sugar, salt, and butter in a large mixing bowl. Cut the mixture until there are lumps the size of small peas.
3. Melt the chocolate morsels. Let cool for approximately 5 minutes, then add the milk and egg and mix well. Beat into the flour mixture, mixing thoroughly.
4. Spread the pie filling in a 2-quart casserole dish. Randomly drop the chocolate batter over the filling, then sprinkle with nuts.

5. Bake for 40–45 minutes. Serve it with a vanilla ice cream if desired.

Nutrition:

Calories: 502

Fat: 1.8 g

Carbs: 10. 2 g

Protein: 19.0 g

Sodium: 265 mg

98. Chocolate Pecan Pie

Preparation Time: 10 minutes

Cooking time: 50 minutes

Servings: 8

Ingredients:

- 3 eggs
- ½ cup sugar
- 1 cup corn syrup
- ½ teaspoon salt
- 1 teaspoon vanilla extract
- ¼ cup melted butter
- 1 cup pecans
- 3 tablespoons semisweet chocolate chips
- 1 unbaked pie shell

Directions:

1. Preheat the oven to 350°F.
2. Beat the eggs plus sugar in a mixing bowl, then add the corn syrup, salt, vanilla, and butter.
3. Put the chocolate chips and pecans inside the pie shell and pour the egg mixture over the top.
4. Bake for 50–60 minutes or until set. Serve with vanilla ice cream.

Nutrition:

Calories: 483

Fat: 13.8 g

Carbs: 22. 2 g

Protein: 29.7 g

Sodium: 154 mg

99. Pumpkin Custard with Gingersnaps

Preparation Time: 30 minutes

Cooking time: 35 minutes

Servings: 8

Ingredients:

Custard:

- 8 egg yolks
- 1¾ cups (1 15-ounce can) pure pumpkin puree
- 1¾ cups heavy whipping cream
- ½ cup of sugar
- 1½ teaspoons pumpkin pie spice
- 1 teaspoon vanilla

Topping:

- 1 cup crushed gingersnap cookies
- 1 tablespoon melted butter
- Whipped Cream:
- 1 cup heavy whipping cream
- 1 tablespoon superfine sugar (or regular sugar if you have no caster sugar)
- ½ teaspoon pumpkin pie spice

Garnish:

- 8 whole gingersnap cookies

Directions:

1. Preheat the oven to 350°F.
2. Separate the yolks from 8 eggs and whisk them together in a large mixing bowl until they are well blended and creamy.

3. Add the pumpkin, sugar, vanilla, heavy cream, and pumpkin pie spice and whisk to combine.

4. Cook the custard batter in a double boiler, stirring until it has thickened enough to coats a spoon.

5. Put the batter into individual custard cups or an 8×8-inch baking pan and bake for about 20 minutes if using individual cups or 30–35 minutes for the baking pan until it is set.

6. Meanwhile, make the topping by combining the crushed gingersnaps and melted butter. After the custard has been in the oven for 15 minutes, sprinkle the gingersnap mixture over the top.

7. When the custard has passed the clean knife test, remove from the oven, and cool to room temperature.

8. Whisk the heavy cream and pumpkin pie spice together with the caster sugar and beat just until it thickens.

9. Serve the custard with the whipped cream and garnish each serving with a gingersnap.

Nutrition:

Calories: 243

Fat: 6.8 g

Carbs: 13. 2 g

Protein: 17.0 g

Sodium: 313 mg

100. Peach Cobbler

Preparation Time: 10 minutes

Cooking time: 45 minutes

Servings: 4

Ingredients:

- 1¼ cups Bisquick
- 1 cup milk
- ½ cup melted butter
- ¼ teaspoon nutmeg
- ½ teaspoon cinnamon
- Vanilla ice cream, for serving

Filling:

- 1 (30-ounce) can peach in syrup, drained
- ¼ cup of sugar

Topping:

- ½ cup brown sugar
- ¼ cup almond slices
- ½ tsp cinnamon
- 1 tbsp melted butter

Directions:

1. Warm-up the oven to 375°F. Oiled the bottom of an 8×8-inch pan.

2. Mix the Bisquick, butter, nutmeg, milk, plus cinnamon in a mixing bowl. Then put into the greased baking pan.

3. Mix the peaches plus sugar in another mixing bowl. Put the filling over the batter in the pan—Bake for about 45 minutes.

4. In another bowl, mix the almonds, cinnamon, brown sugar, plus melted butter.

5. Once done cooking, cover evenly with the topping and bake within 10 minutes, then serve it with a scoop of vanilla ice cream.

Nutrition:

Calories: 446

Fat: 12.6 g

Carbs: 21. 2 g

Protein: 21.1 g

Sodium: 300 mg

101. Royal Dansk Butter Cookies

Preparation Time: 15 minutes

Cooking Time: 25 minutes

Servings: 10

Ingredients:

- 120g cake flour sifted
- ½ teaspoon vanilla extract
- 25g powdered sugar
- 120g softened butter, at room temperature
- A pinch of sea salt, approximately ¼ teaspoon

Directions:

1. Beat the butter with sugar, vanilla, and salt until almost doubled in mass and lightened to a yellowish-white color using a hand mixer, for 8 to 10 minutes, on low to medium speed.

2. Scrape the mixture from the sides of your bowl using a rubber spatula. Sift the flour x 3 times & gently fold in until well incorporated.

3. Transfer the batter into a sheet of plastic wrap, roll into a log & cut a hole on it, placing it into the piping bag attached with a nozzle flower tip 4.6cm/1.81" x 1.18".

4. Pipe each cookie into 5cm wide swirls on a parchment paper-lined baking tray.

5. Cover & place them in a freezer until firm up for 30 minutes.

6. Preheat your oven to 300 F in advance. Once done, bake until the edges start to turn golden, for 20 minutes.

7. Let completely cool on the cooling rack before serving. Store them in an airtight container.

Nutrition:

Calories: 220

Fat: 8.8 g

Carbs: 22. 3 g

Protein: 30.2 g

Sodium: 200 mg

Conclusion

We hope it was informative and provided you with all of the tools you need to achieve your goals, making the most delicious 'take-out' in your kitchen. The next move is to collect all the necessary ingredients to make delicious meals and treats.

You will also need to understand and know how to store your masterpiece selections properly. For meals scheduled to be eaten at least three days after cooking, freezing is a great option. Freezing food is safe and convenient, but it doesn't work for every type of meal. You can also freeze the ingredients for a slow cooker meal and then dump out the container into the slow cooker and leave it there. It saves a lot of time and means you can pre-prep meals up to one to two months in advance.

You must also know and understand the proper ways to reheat your meals. Most people opt to microwave their meals for warming, but you can use any other conventional heating source in your kitchen as well. However, you have to be careful with microwaving because over-cooking can cause food to taste bad.

To combat this, cook your food in one-minute intervals and check on it between each minute. You can also help your food cook more evenly and quickly but keeping your meat cut into small pieces when you cook it. You should never put food directly from the freezer into the microwave. Let your frozen food thaw first when it's possible.

Food reheating and prep safety will become second nature over time. However, mistakes do happen, and as such, it's best to cook for short periods rather than longer ones, so you have less of a risk of making a mistake and needing to scrap everything you have prepared for that substantial amount of time. While it is a lot and seems complicated, meals prepping is the best way to set yourself up for success using your delicious copycat recipes. Make the meals using double the products and adjust the times; that is all it is to it!

Don't store hot food in the fridge. Keep your refrigerator at the proper temperature (should be below 40° Fahrenheit). If your refrigerator is warmer than this, it promotes the growth of bacteria. Any drastic temperature changes will cause condensation to form on the food items. You need to let your prepared food cool down in the open air - before placing it in a container, then closing the lid. The increased moisture levels can open the door to bacteria growth.

There are some other things you have to consider when freezing your meals. You should always label your container with the date that you put it in the freezer. You also need to double-check that your bottles, jars, or bags are each sealed tightly. If your containers aren't air-tight, your food will become freezer burnt and need to be trashed. We hope these additional suggestions will make your Copycat Recipes a treasured item in beside you.

Lastly, never stop yourself from the fear of mistakes or errors, as they are common. Enjoy cooking these meals as much as you enjoy having them. We, too, have given these recipes several trials only to master them. So better give it a try, and share it with others to inspire them all.

Why not get started right now? Have fun, and enjoy the time and money saved cooking at home!